RA
2001
Suppl.

For Your Health
A Study Guide and Self-Assessment Workbook

Gordon Edlin

John A. Burns School of Medicine
University of Hawaii, Manoa Campus
Honolulu, Hawaii

Eric Golanty

Las Positas College
Livermore, California

JONES AND BARTLETT PUBLISHERS
Sudbury, Massachusetts

BOSTON   TORONTO   LONDON   SINGAPORE

KVCC WITHDRAWN
KALAMAZOO VALLEY
COMMUNITY COLLEGE
LIBRARY

World Headquarters
Jones and Bartlett Publishers
40 Tall Pine Drive
Sudbury, MA 01776
978-443-5000
info@jbpub.com
www.jbpub.com

Jones and Bartlett Publishers Canada
6339 Ormindale Way
Mississauga, Ontario L5V 1J2
CANADA

Jones and Bartlett Publishers International
Barb House, Barb Mews
London W6 7PA
UK

Jones and Bartlett's books and products are available through most bookstores and online booksellers. To contact Jones and Bartlett Publishers directly, call 800-832-0034, fax 978-443-8000, or visit our website, www.jbpub.com.

Substantial discounts on bulk quantities of Jones and Bartlett's publications are available to corporations, professional associations, and other qualified organizations. For details and specific discount information, contact the special sales department at Jones and Bartlett via the above contact information or send an email to specialsales@jbpub.com.

Copyright © 2007 by Jones and Bartlett Publishers, Inc.

All rights reserved. No part of the material protected by this copyright may be reproduced or utilized in any form, electronic or mechanical, including photocopying, recording, or by any information storage and retrieval system, without written permission from the copyright owner.

Production Credits
Acquisitions Editor: Jacqueline Mark-Geraci
Production Editor: Karen C. Ferreira
Editorial Assistant: Amy L. Flagg
Associate Marketing Manager: Wendy Thayer
Manufacturing Buyer: Therese Connell
Interior Design: Anne Spencer
Composition: Shepherd, Inc.
Cover Design: Kristin E. Ohlin
Cover Image: © Losevsky Pavel/ShutterStock, Inc.
Printing and Binding: Courier Stoughton
Cover Printing: Courier Stoughton

ISBN-13: 978-0-7637-4344-4
ISBN-10: 0-7637-4344-5

Printed in the United States of America
10 09 08 07   10 9 8 7 6 5 4 3 2

Contents

1 Achieving Personal Health 1

1.1 My Definition of Health   1

1.2 Health Issues Affecting My Academic Performance   3

1.3 My Campus Health Environment   5

1.4 My Health and Wellness Assessment   7

1.5 My Health Behaviors   11

1.6 My Personal Vital Statistics   13

1.7 Health Behavior Change Project   15

2 Mind-Body Communications Maintain Wellness 19

2.1 The Relaxation Response   19

2.2 Autogenic Training   21

2.3 Anchoring   23

2.4 Image Visualization   25

2.5 Progressive Muscle Relaxation   27

2.6 Massage   29

2.7 Leaving It at the River   31

3 Managing Stress: Restoring Mind-Body Harmony 33

3.1 My Stressors   33

3.2 My Stress Reactions   35

3.3 How Susceptible Am I to Stress?   37

3.4 Warning Signs of Stress   39

3.5 My Life Changes and Stress   41

3.6 Prioritizing Tasks: First Things First   43

3.7 Time Audit for Time Management   45

3.8 Are You a Procrastinator?   47

3.9 Image Visualization for Exam Anxiety   49

4 Mental Health and Mental Illness 51

4.1 Saying No   51

4.2 My Definition of Mental Health   53

4.3 Keeping a Journal   55

4.4 My Fears and Phobias   57

4.5 My Sleep and Dream Record   59

4.6 How Can I Sleep Better?   61

4.7 How Do I Affect Others?   63

5 Choosing a Nutritious Diet 65

5.1 My Estimated Daily Calorie Requirement   65

5.2. My Food Diary   67

5.3 My Dietary Analysis   69

5.4 Fast-Food Restaurant Research   71

5.5 Can I Read a Food Label?   73

6 Managing a Healthy Weight 75

6.1 My Body Weight   75

6.2 My Body Image   77

7 Physical Activity for Health and Well-Being 79

7.1 My Target Heart Rate   79

7.2 My Fitness Index   81

7.3 My Flexibility Index   83

7.4 The Sun Salute   85

8 Sexuality and Intimate Relationships 87

8.1 Sexual Anatomy   87

8.2 My Sexual Attitudes   99

8.3 My Sexual Values   101

8.4 Sexual Communication   103

8.5 My Attitudes About Love   105

8.6 My Relationship Wants and Needs   107

8.7 My Relationship Values   109

8.8 Listening Exercise   111

9 Understanding Pregnancy and Parenthood 113

9.1 Parenthood and Me   113

10 Choosing a Fertility Control Method 115

10.1 Contraception   115

10.2 Choosing a Contraceptive   117

11 **Protecting Against Sexually Transmitted Diseases and AIDS** 119
  11.1 AIDS and Me   119

12 **Reducing Infections and Building Immunity: Knowledge Encourages Prevention** 121
  12.1 My Vaccination Record   121

13 **Cancer: Understanding Risks and Means of Prevention** 123
  13.1 My Cancer Risks   123
  13.2 My Environmental Cancer Risks   125

14 **Cardiovascular Diseases: Understanding Risks and Measures of Prevention** 127
  14.1 My Risk for Heart Disease   127

15 **Heredity and Disease** 129
  15.1 My Family Medical History   129

16 **Using Drugs Responsibly** 131
  16.1 Being Knowledgeable About Drugs   131
  16.2 Medicines I Take   133
  16.3 Nonessential Drugs I Consume   135
  16.4 Drugs in Media and Advertising   137

17 **Eliminating Tobacco Use** 139
  17.1 Why Do I Smoke?   139
  17.2 Am I Addicted to Nicotine?   143

18 **Using Alcohol Responsibly** 145
  18.1 My Alcohol Use   145
  18.2 Cutting Down on Drinking   147

19 **Making Decisions About Health Care** 149
  19.1 My Medical History   149
  19.2 Am I an Intelligent Health Consumer?   151
  19.3 Using the Internet for Health Research   153
  19.4 Web Field Trips   155

20 **Exploring Alternative Medicines** 157
  20.1 Exploring Complementary and Alternative Medicine   157

21 **Accidents and Injuries** 159
  21.1 Preventing Intentional Injury   159
  21.2 Preventing Unintentional Injury   161

22 **Understanding Aging and Dying** 163
  22.1 Healthy Aging   163

23 **Violence in Our Society** 165
  23.1 Do I Protect Myself from Crime?   165

24 **Working Toward a Healthy Environment** 167
  24.1 Environmental Awareness Questionnaire   167
  24.2 How Environmentally Friendly Is My Car?   169
  24.3 How Healthy Is My Drinking Water?   171

Preface

As a supplement to the *Health and Wellness* textbook, this workbook offers two kinds of activities that guide you to improve and enhance your health and well-being:

1. Self-assessment questionnaires, which enable you to learn about and assess aspects of your health.
2. Skill-building activities, which direct you in adopting healthy behaviors.

Self-assessments are fun and interesting. You get to learn something about yourself. Each item in a self-assessment teaches you something about the topic that the assessment is addressing. Knowledge about oneself is the basis of change. Knowledge of a health topic provides the specific goals for change.

Skill-building activities are fun and motivating. They also can be work because they ask you not only to assess yourself and set health goals, but to change something you habitually do, which isn't necessarily easy. You're good at what you practice, so if you've been thinking or doing something a certain way for a while, it probably feels like "second nature" to you, and anything new feels uncomfortable or strange. That is the reason that skill-building requires a feasible plan comprised of small steps, time, and patience to develop the skill.

When changing a health behavior, you are bound to encounter obstacles. When you do, consider the following:

1. Obstacles always arise. So when they do, rather than getting so disappointed and frustrated that you give up, keep your goals in mind and when you can, pick up the project again. Think of how Martin Luther King, Jr. and Gandhi overcame their obstacles. They kept their eyes on the prize and moved ahead as they could.
2. Obstacles are full of information. They tell you how the world works instead of how you wish it would work. They ask you to consider if your goals are worth the effort. They ask you to consider if your strategy for accomplishing a goal is feasible. They ask you to be compassionate to yourself and others who experience disappointment and frustration.
3. Bravery is not the absence of fear. Bravery is acknowledging your fear, "being" with your fear, and then proceeding as best you can even though you are afraid.

Each activity in the workbook is introduced by a quotation. In addition to doing the specific activity, think about and possibly write your interpretation of the quotation. What does it mean to you?

We hope you find the activities in this workbook interesting, enjoyable, and beneficial.

Gordon Edlin and Eric Golanty
Authors of *Health and Wellness*

1.1 My Definition of Health

Whatever you can do or dream you can do, begin it. Boldness has genius, power, and magic in it.
—Goethe

Directions

Write a one-paragraph response to these questions:

- What is your personal definition of health?

_____

_____

_____

_____

_____

_____

_____

_____

- How does your definition compare to the World Health Organization's definition of health (Chapter 1)?

_____

_____

_____

_____

_____

_____

_____

1.2 Health Issues Affecting My Academic Performance

You're good at what you practice.
—Sensei Mel Weitsman,
Berkeley Zen Center

Directions

1. Use the chart below to indicate how much each health issue affects you.

2. For any frequent health issue, describe how it affects your academic performance and offer strategies for lessening the frequency with which the issue

occurs.

Health Issue	Affects My Academic Performance		
	Rarely/not at all	Sometimes	Frequently
Stress	_____	_____	_____
Cold/flu/sore throat	_____	_____	_____
Sleep difficulties	_____	_____	_____
Concern about family/friend	_____	_____	_____
Relationship difficulties	_____	_____	_____
Depression/anxiety	_____	_____	_____
Internet use/games	_____	_____	_____
Sinus infection	_____	_____	_____
Death of friend/family	_____	_____	_____
Alcohol use	_____	_____	_____

1.3 My Campus Health Environment

Even if you're on the right track, you'll get run over if you just sit there.
—Will Rogers

Directions

The following chart lists health goals for American colleges and universities for year 2010 and baseline data from year 2000. Rate *your perception* of your school's efforts toward achieving each of the listed 2010 health goals. Mark "thumbs up" if you perceive your school as working toward the 2010 health goal. Mark "thumbs down" if you perceive that it is not working toward the 2010 health goal.

Health Goal	Year 2000 Data	Year 2010 Goal	👍	👎
Increase the proportion of college students with health insurance.	83.3%	100%		
Increase the proportion of college students receiving information from their institution on each of 11 priority health-risk behavior areas.*	3.1%	17.4		
Increase the proportion of females who use contraception.	95.1%	100%		
Reduce unintentional pregnancies among college women.	25.3%	17.5%		
Increase the proportion of sexually active women/men who used condoms at last intercourse.	40/46.8%	60/60%		
Increase use of safety belts.	69.5%	94%		
Decrease the proportion of college students who have been in an emotionally abusive relationship (per 1,000).	124	93.9		
Reduce the annual rate of rape or attempted rape (per 1,000).	34.6	23.3		
Reduce sexual assault/unwanted sexual touching other than rape (per 1,000).	96	56.4		
Reduce physical assaults (per 1,000).	37	21.3		
Reduce the proportion of college students who report that they drove after drinking any alcohol at all during the previous 30 days.	30.9%	15.3%		
Reduce the proportion of college students engaging in high-risk (binge) drinking of alcoholic beverages during the past two weeks.	39%	20%		
Reduce tobacco use by college students.	25.1%	10.5%		
Reduce the rate of suicide attempts by adolescents and college students (12-month average rate).	1.5%	0.53%		
Increase the proportion of adults and college students who are at a healthy weight. Healthy weight is defined as a body mass index (BMI) equal to or greater than 18.5 and less than 25.	66.8%	75%		
Increase the proportion of college students who consume at least five daily servings of fruit and vegetables.	7.4%	25.5%		
Increase the proportion of adults and college students who use the oral health care system each year.	77%	92%		

*11 priority health-risk behaviors: tobacco use, alcohol use, sexual assault/relationship violence, violence prevention, injury prevention and safety, suicide prevention, pregnancy prevention, HIV/AIDS prevention, STD prevention, dietary behaviors and nutrition, physical activity and fitness

Source: American College Health Association - National College Health Assessment, 2003.

1.5 My Health Behaviors

He has half the deed done who has made a beginning.
—Horace

Health is a precious gift that you give yourself by living meaningfully and in harmony with your inner self and all that surrounds you. Researchers have found that the personal behaviors listed in the table below contribute to health.

Directions

1. List the behaviors in the table that are regular aspects of your life.

   _____

   _____

   _____

   _____

2. Identify one behavior that you would like to be part of your life right now and explain your reasoning. Consider doing a Health Behavior Change project (see workbook Exercise 1.7) to integrate one of these health behaviors into your life.

   _____

   _____

   _____

The Breslow Study	The Ornish Study
No smoking	No smoking
7–8 hours of sleep per night	No more than 10% of daily calories from fat
Body weight not less than 10% and not more than 30% of recommended for height and body frame	Daily meditation
Regular exercise	Daily exercise
Eating breakfast regularly	Vegetarian diet
Little between-meal snacking	Daily yoga
Little or no alcohol consumption (1–2 drinks per day)	Support group meetings twice a week

Note: The data in column 1 are from L. Breslow and J. E. Enstrom, 1980, "Persistence of health habits and their relationship to mortality," *Preventive Medicine, 9,* 469–483; T. C. Camacho and J. A. Wiley, 1983, Health practices, social networks, and change in physical health. In L. Berkman and L. Breslow, eds., *Health and Ways of Living: The Alameda County Study.* New York: Oxford University Press. Data in column 2 are from D. Ornish et al., 1998, "Intensive lifestyle changes for reversal of coronary heart disease," *Journal of the American Medical Association, 280,* 2001–2007.

1.6 My Personal Vital Statistics

Your health is bound to be affected if day after day you say the opposite of what you feel.
—Boris Pasternak, *Doctor Zhivago*

Enter the appropriate data about yourself. Date it and keep it for your personal records.

Height in inches (without shoes):_____

Weight in pounds (with clothes):_____

Highest adult weight:_____ pounds. At what age?_____

Lowest adult weight:_____ pounds. At what age? _____

Recommended weight for height (see text, Chapter 5):_____

Body Mass Index (see text, Chapter 5):_____

Resting heart rate (pulse): _____beats per minute (see Exercise 7.1)

Blood pressure: Systolic (top number): _____ Diastolic (bottom number): _____

Blood type: | A | B | O | AB | Rh− | Rh+ |

Total blood cholesterol: _____ LDL cholesterol: _____ HDL cholesterol: _____

1.7 Health Behavior Change Project

Everyone has the power for greatness, not fame, but greatness. Because greatness is determined by service.

—Martin Luther King, Jr.

Design, carry out, and evaluate a project for changing a personal health behavior (e.g.: stop smoking, learn a relaxation method, alter diet, begin an exercise plan).

The Health Behavior Change project has five steps:

Step 1. Project Declaration: You state what you want to do. Address the following:

1. The reasons for your choice

2. What you hope to learn or achieve and why

3. Any prior experiences that are similar

4. Your start and stop dates

5. The ways you will determine progress

Step 2. Research: You find four resources that provide information about your proposed Health Behavior Change project. Consult books, magazines, the Internet, or personal advisors to determine a way(s) to accomplish your goal(s). Because research in the health field is extensive, find resources that are no older than five years. For each of the four resources report the following:

- The title

- The author or writer

- The source: name of magazine, producer of video, affiliation of professional expert, Internet address

- Date of publication and pages on which the information appears

Step 3. Project Plan: You develop and describe a plan for carrying out your Health Behavior Change project. Describe what you plan to do for your Health Behavior Change project and the ways you will determine progress.

Step 4. Project Activity: You carry out your project for three weeks. Choose a start date. Keep a diary/journal of your activity. Note obstacles that get in the way of progress. At the end of each week, write a progress report that summarizes that week's experience, including obstacles you encounter.

Step 5. Assessment: You write an evaluation of your experience by:

- Summarizing your project plan and the health principles it represented

- Describing the experience of trying to accomplish your goal(s)

- Listing at least two things about your topic that you learned

- Describing what doing the project helped you learn about yourself

- Describing what you learned about how to change a health behavior

- Stating whether the project was worthwhile and why

Example Health Behavior Change Projects

The following are suggestions for Health Behavior change projects.

Stop Smoking
Quiet Time Exploration
Putting Exercise into Your Life
Five-A-Day
Dietary Fiber Consumption
Increase Your Physical Fitness
Weight Management
Increase Your Flexibility
Dietary Fat Reduction

Stop Smoking

Quitting smoking is a process, not an event. Whereas a few ex-smokers quit by waking up one morning and tossing out their cigarettes, most ex-smokers think about quitting for a while before they try to stop. Also, whereas "cold turkey" is one way to quit, smoking addiction is so powerful that success at quitting is more likely when you follow a plan. The goal of this project is to learn about the quitting process and to develop a personal plan for quitting.

Begin your project by checking out the stop-smoking web page on the Health and Wellness Web site (http://health.jbpub.com/hwonline/9e/workbook/smoking.cfm). Note the links to online stop-smoking programs. In your project declaration, answer these questions:

1. What is your age?

2. How long have you been smoking?

3. How many cigarettes do you currently smoke each day?

4. What pleasures do you get from smoking?

5. What are the reasons you are choosing this project?

6. Have you ever tried to stop smoking? If so, what happened?

7. Do you have access to a doctor or other health care provider?

8. What is your opinion of medications that help people to stop smoking?

Quiet Time Exploration

For three weeks, experiment with different methods of relaxation to find one(s) that suits you and that you can practice indefinitely to enhance your health and well-being.

During Week 1

Experiment with three of the following relaxation techniques (or others of your choosing).

- Mantra meditation

- Breathing meditation

- Walking

- T'ai chi ch'uan

- Image visualization

- Progressive muscle relaxation

- Hatha yoga

During Week 2

Choose one technique and practice it for at least 3 days for 10 minutes each time.

During Week 3

Practice your chosen technique for at least 6 days for 20 minutes each day. For each day record the following information:

- The name the relaxation activity you're doing

- The time you spent each day doing the activity

- What you experienced doing the activity

- Any obstacles that prevented you from carrying out a day's activity

- Strategies for overcoming any obstacles

Putting Exercise into Your Life

1. Use your Time Audit (see Exercise 3.7) to identify four "windows" of time during the week to exercise.

2. Choose an activity that interests you and schedule it for your four "exercise windows".

3. Keep a diary of your exercise sessions. For each day record the following information:

    - The activity

    - The time you spent doing the activity

    - What you experienced while doing the activity

    - Any obstacles that prevented you from carrying out a day's activity

    - Strategies for overcoming any obstacles

4. Make a graph in which you record the number of sessions of exercise and their length each week.

Five-A-Day

Use your Food Diary (see Exercise 5.2) to determine the number of servings of fruits and vegetables you consume each day. For three weeks, try to increase by one (at most two) the number of servings a day of fruits and vegetables that you consume.

1. Keep a daily record of the number of servings of fruits and vegetables you consume.

2. Make a graph in which you record the number of servings of fruits and vegetables you consume each day over the three-week activity period.

3. Identify any obstacles that prevented you from carrying out a day's activity.

4. Develop strategies for overcoming any obstacles that keep you from increasing the number of servings you consume.

Dietary Fiber Consumption

1. Use your Food Diary (see Exercise 5.2) to determine the number of grams of fiber you typically consume per day.

2. Make a list of foods that you will consume to bring your total number of grams of fiber consumed to 20–30 per day.

3. For three weeks, try to consume 20–30 grams of fiber per day. Keep a diary in which you

    - Record the number of grams of fiber you consume and their sources

    - Identify obstacles that prevented you from achieving your goal

    - Identify and implement strategies for overcoming obstacles

4. Record on a graph the number of grams of fiber you consume daily over the three-week activity period.

Increase Your Physical Fitness

1. Measure your level of fitness using the Harvard Step Test (see Exercise 7.2).

2. Measure your resting heart rate.

3. Determine your Target Zone heart rate (see Exercise 7.1).

4. Refer to your Time Audit to find at least four times per week when you can exercise for 30–60 minutes (see Exercise 3.7).

    My Fitness Index is _____.

    My resting heart rate is _____ beats per minute.

    My Target Zone heart rate is between _____ and _____ beats per minute.

5. Choose an aerobic activity that interests you and exercise at least four times a week for three weeks. Determine your heart rate at the end of each exercise session to see if you are exercising within your target zone.

6. Keep a diary of your activity. For each day record the following information:

    - The activity

    - The time you spent doing the activity

    - What you experienced doing the activity

    - Any obstacles that prevented you from carrying out a day's activity

    - Strategies for overcoming any obstacles

7. For each week record your resting heart rate and your Fitness Index.

8. Make a graph in which you record for the three-week period:

    - The number of sessions of exercise and their length

    - Your resting heart rate at the start and end of the project

    - Your Fitness Index at the start and end of the project

Weight Management

Develop a plan for weight loss/weight management.

1. Determine your healthy weight range by consulting the weight-for-height tables and BMI table in Chapter 5 of the text.

    My healthful body weight range is _____.

    My Body Mass Index is _____.

2. If you wish to lose weight, make a plan that combines increased exercise and moderate calorie reduction to produce the loss of not more than one pound a week until body weight is reduced by 10%. List the types and duration of exercise you will do, foods that you will limit, and the length of time you will devote to a weight loss regime.

   Exercise I will increase:

   _____

   _____

   _____

   Foods I will limit:

   _____

   _____

   _____

   Time allotted to lose 10% of current body weight:

   _____

   _____

   _____

3. Increase exercise and limit certain foods (e.g., junk and fast foods, sodas).

4. Keep a daily record of exercise and dietary changes. For each day record the following information:
   - The exercise changes you're doing
   - The food changes you make
   - What you experience
   - Any obstacles that prevented you from carrying out a day's plan
   - Strategies for overcoming any obstacles

5. Make a graph in which you record each day the number of minutes of exercise you do and the number of calories you don't consume.

Increase Your Flexibility
Increase your flexibility by undertaking a regular regime of stretching or yoga.

1. Measure your flexibility by using the YMCA flexibility test (see Exercise 7.3).

2. Refer to your Time Audit (see Exercise 3.7) to find at least four occasions per week when you can stretch for 10–20 minutes each time.

3. Choose a stretching regime (see text Chapter 7) that interests you and carry it out at least four times a week.

4. Keep a diary of your activity:
   - Record the number of stretching sessions you do each week.
   - Record the time spent in each session.
   - Record your physical and psychological experiences before and after each session.
   - Identify any obstacles that prevented you from carrying out a day's activity.
   - Develop strategies for overcoming any obstacles.

5. Make a graph in which you record the number of sessions of stretching each week. Determine your flexibility index (inches reached) at the end of each week.

Dietary Fat Reduction
Reduce fat consumption to 30% (or less) of daily calories.

1. Use your Food Diary and The U.S. Department of Agriculture's Nutrient Data Laboratory Web site (http://www.ars.usda.gov/ba/bhnrc/ndl) to determine the percentage of calories of fat you typically consume each day.

2. Make a list of food exchanges that you will employ to lower your fat intake (e.g., piece of fruit for a candy bar, pasta for a hamburger, etc.).

3. For three weeks, alter your diet to lower your fat intake.

4. Keep a dairy in which you record the following information:
   - The amount of fat grams & fat calories you consume each day
   - Any obstacles that prevented you from carrying out a day's activity
   - Strategies for overcoming any obstacles

5. Make a graph in which you record the percentage of daily calories derived from fat during the three-week action period.

CHAPTER

2

2.1 The Relaxation Response

Everything starts with clear intention.
—Yvonne Rand,
Buddhist priest and teacher

Many students live fast-paced, hectic lives that are full of time pressures and stress. Trying to accommodate to all of life's demands produces near continuous physiologic arousal, resulting in sleep disturbances, muscle tension, gastrointestinal symptoms, and an increased risk for cardiovascular disease. The Relaxation Response is an automatic physiological pattern opposing nervous system arousal. Do it for 10 to 20 minutes each day to keep yourself centered and calm.

Directions

1. Place yourself in an environment in which you are comfortable and can relax. Turn off cell phones, pagers, computers, and music. Lock the door.

2. Sit or lie comfortably. Breathe comfortably.

3. Silently repeat the word *one.* If your mind wanders, as soon as you notice, refocus your attention on silently repeating the word *one.* Do not become angry or frustrated because you "aren't doing it right."

4. Do the exercise for as long as you are able. Try to work up to 20 minutes per day.

2.2 Autogenic Training

···

An ounce of example is worth a pound of advice.
—Evan Esar

Autogenic training uses autosuggestion to balance and harmonize the mind and body. Autogenic training involves concentrating on one of six basic autogenic phrases for a few minutes each day for a week or more. After weeks or months of practice, you are able to attain a deep sense of relaxation, often within seconds. The six basic autosuggestions are as follows:

- My arms and legs are heavy.

- My arms and legs are warm.

- My heartbeat is calm and regular.

- My lungs breathe me.

- My abdomen is warm.

- My forehead is cool.

Directions

1. Place yourself in an environment in which you are comfortable and can relax. Turn off cell phones, pagers, computers, and music. Lock the door.

2. Sit or lie comfortably. Breathe comfortably.

3. Choose one of the autogenic phrases from the preceding list and silently (or aloud) repeat it seven times.

4. Open your eyes, stretch, and mentally note or "observe" the sensations in your body.

5. Repeat steps 3 and 4 five times, for a total of about 10 minutes.

6. After one week, carry out the exercise using a different autogenic phrase.

Note: The exact phrasing of any autogenic suggestion is not critical to its effectiveness. The words carry no particular power. Any suggestion can be rephrased so that it becomes comfortable, believable, and acceptable to you.

2.3 Anchoring

Ordinary men hate solitude, but the master makes use of it, embracing his aloneness, realizing he is one with the whole universe.
—Lao Tzu

Follow the directions below to learn how to Anchor. Then, on each of six consecutive days, practice Anchoring for 20 minutes. At the end of the six days, describe your experience. You can also check out the online Anchoring tutorial at http://health.jbpub.com/hwonline/9e/workbook/anchoring.cfm

Directions

Become comfortable: Sit straight, uncross your legs, place your feet flat on the floor. Place your hands in your lap and take two easy, deep breaths. Then breathe easily and naturally. Bring your shoulders down from your ears.

Step 1.   Anchoring on the feet: Close your eyes for a few seconds and focus your awareness on the sensation of the bottoms of your feet touching the insoles of your shoes. After you open your eyes, note what your mind was doing while your eyes were closed.

Step 2.   Anchoring on the back: Close your eyes for a few seconds and focus your awareness on the sensation of your back touching the chair. After a couple of seconds with your eyes closed, open your eyes, take an easy breath, and note what your mind was doing while your eyes were closed.

Step 3.   Anchoring on the breath: Close your eyes for a few seconds and notice your breathing. Don't change your breathing rhythm or pattern, just notice the breath going in and out of your body.

Now you know three basic Anchoring postures: feet on the floor, back against the chair, and focusing on the breath. With a bit of practice, you will discover the Anchoring posture that is best for you.

Step 4.   Anchoring for 30 seconds, and then 90 seconds: Become comfortable (see above). Choose one of the three Anchoring postures as your Anchor place. Close your eyes, and focus your awareness on your Anchor place for 30 seconds. While you're Anchoring, if you notice your mind wandering, refocus your awareness on your Anchor place. When you think the 30 seconds has elapsed, open your eyes and take a breath.

What did you notice while you were Anchoring? Did you hear sounds? Did your mind wander? Did you think about your to-do list? Did you tell yourself this was silly? Did you feel sleepy? Did you relax? All of these reactions are common. Whenever you Anchor, you can expect your mind to wander and to think. When you notice that it does, just notice, and refocus your awareness on your Anchor place. When you are ready, try Anchoring for 90 seconds.

2.4 Image Visualization

A wise man changes his mind. A fool, never.
—Spanish proverb

Your mind has the power to promote your personal wellness and to help healing. By dwelling on negative thoughts and images, such as "I feel lousy," you increase the chance that you will feel that way. On the other hand, thinking positive thoughts, such as "I feel great" or "Today is a good day," you can create positive feelings and positive behavioral outcomes. You can put healing suggestions into your mind, too. For example, you can suggest to yourself that a headache will go away in an hour or a cold will be mild.

Directions

Find a quiet, pleasant place where you can sit or lie down comfortably. Remove any uncomfortable clothing, eyeglasses, or contact lenses. Turn off the phone, TV, and computer. Give yourself permission to relax and decide what you are going to visualize. It's probably best to begin with something specific. You can visualize yourself being slimmer, giving up cigarettes, being successful in an upcoming job interview, or taking an exam while feeling confident and sure of the answers. You can visualize yourself becoming physically stronger or an area of your body becoming well.

Allow your eyes to close, and relax the muscles in the eyelids all the way—to the point where they are so relaxed and comfortable that you feel you are unable to pull your eyelids open. Then let your mind transfer that same comfortable, relaxed feeling to all the other parts of the body, one by one, from top to bottom—head, chest, arms, hands, back, stomach, legs, feet.

Imagine that you are floating on a white cloud bathed in warm sunlight. Everything is quiet and peaceful. You are warm and comfortable and serene. Allow your mind to visualize whatever scene or image it chooses

that is related to what you want to improve or heal. Accept your mind's images. They are helping you to change, to feel better. Allow yourself to remain in this relaxed state while your mind continues to create pleasant, positive, beneficial images. Begin to notice how relaxed your body is and how good it feels.

Whenever your mind decides it wants to return to a fully awake state, you will automatically open your eyes and be fully aware of your surroundings. Notice how refreshed and relaxed you feel!

2.5 Progressive Muscle Relaxation

Meditation is the action of silence.
—Krishnamurti

Developed by American physician Edmund Jacobson in 1938, Progressive Muscle Relaxation (PMR) involves tightening individual muscles or muscle groups for five seconds and slowly releasing to create a reflex relaxation.

Directions

On each of two consecutive days, practice PMR, following the directions below. You can start at your feet and progress toward your head or vice versa, whichever is most comfortable for you. Try voice-recording the directions so you don't have to refer to the printed page. *Note:* Some people experience muscle cramps while doing this exercise, especially in their feet. If a muscle cramps, either (1) straighten out the muscle, or (2) "breathe through" the muscle: close your eyes and imagine that air is entering your body through the tight muscle instead of your lungs. If cramping or any other aspect of this exercise is uncomfortable, you may stop.

PMR Exercise (15–20 minutes)
Phase 1: Sinking into the floor
Put yourself in quiet, comfortable surroundings.
Shoes off, clothes loosened.
Lie on your back on a soft or padded surface.
Set feet slightly apart with palms facing upward.
Close eyes; breathe naturally.
Observe thoughts without focusing on them.
As if it were a sponge, imagine the surface on which you are lying drawing tension from your body. As tension leaves your body, notice that it feels as though you are sinking into the floor.
Breathe naturally.
Lie quietly for at least two minutes.

Phase 2: Lower-body PMR
Focus your awareness on your feet. Breathe normally.
Keeping your heel on the floor, point the toes on your left foot away from you as far as you can. Hold five seconds and slowly release.
Repeat for right foot.
Rest, breathe naturally, and observe the sensation that follows.
Keeping your heel on the floor, point the toes on your left foot toward you as far as you can. Hold five seconds and slowly release.

Repeat for right foot.
Rest, breathe naturally, and observe the sensation that follows.
With leg outstretched, tighten the thigh muscles of your left leg. Hold five seconds and slowly release.
Repeat for right leg.
Rest, breathe naturally, and observe the sensation that follows.
Tense pelvic (butt) muscles. Hold five seconds and slowly release.
Rest, breathe naturally, and observe the sensation that follows.

Phase 3: Upper-body PMR
Tense stomach muscles. Hold five seconds and slowly release.
Rest, breathe naturally, and observe the sensation that follows.
With palms turned down and keeping your forearm on the floor, bend your left hand at the wrist and point the fingers back as far as they will go. Hold five seconds and slowly release.
Repeat for right hand.
Rest, breathe naturally, and observe the sensation that follows.
With palms turned up and keeping your forearm on the floor, bend your left hand at the wrist and point the fingers toward your face as far as they will go. Hold five seconds and slowly release.
Repeat for right hand.
Rest, breathe naturally, and observe the sensation that follows.
Tense muscles of the left upper arm. Hold five seconds and slowly release.
Repeat for right arm.
Rest, breathe naturally, and observe the sensation that follows.
Tense the muscles in your back. Hold five seconds and slowly release.
Rest, breathe naturally, and observe the sensation that follows.
Tense the muscles in your shoulders.
Hold five seconds and slowly release.
Rest, breathe naturally, and observe the sensation that follows.

Phase 4: Head and neck PMR
Tense the muscles in your neck. Hold five seconds and slowly release.
Rest, breathe naturally, and observe the sensation that follows.
Tense the muscles in your face. Hold five seconds and slowly release.
Rest, breathe naturally, and observe the sensation that follows.
Close your eyes and squeeze the lids tightly shut. Hold five seconds and slowly release.
Rest, breathe naturally, and observe the sensation that follows.

2.6 Massage

I am not who I think I am.
I am not who you think I am.
I am who I think you think I am.
—Anonymous

Everyone experiences tense muscles and soreness in parts of the body occasionally. Some parts of the body, such as the neck, shoulders, and back, are prime locations for accumulated tension. Mental and emotional distress can cause muscle tension and physical discomfort.

Massage is an excellent way to reduce physical tension and relax body muscles. In turn, a relaxed body facilitates a relaxed state of mind. All human beings need physical contact with other people. Babies and children are constantly seeking ways to be held, touched, and massaged by their caregivers. Mothers instinctively stroke and rub their infants. Unfortunately, as we grow older we tend to give and receive less physical contact.

Giving a Back Massage

Anyone can give a massage to another person. All that's required is the desire to make another person feel more comfortable and a willingness to be sensitive to another person's stiff muscles.

Learn by exchanging massages with friends and persons you are comfortable with and trust. The person being massaged can be sitting up or lying down. The area to be massaged should be free of clothing. Begin with the neck, using your thumbs to press the muscles on either side of the spine. Press firmly and smoothly away from the spine. Work down the back, always pressing down and away from the spine. Be sensitive to sore places or knots of tense muscles. Apply steady gentle pressure to these areas until you feel the person relax or the muscles soften. As you become more experienced, you can use the heels of your hands or your knuckles to knead tense muscles. Always be sensitive to what the other person is feeling.

It helps to use a small amount of massage oil on your hands to reduce friction. You may want to play soft music or encourage the person to relax while you are massaging him or her.

Giving a Foot Massage

A foot massage is a relaxing, pleasant experience. The foot is a sensitive part of the body and often has places that are stiff or sore. Most people feel greatly relaxed after receiving a foot massage.

Begin by washing the person's feet with warm water. Rub the whole foot and ankle with a small amount of massage oil. Massage each toe and between each toe. Gently pull each toe to stretch the muscles and joints. You may hear the joint make a small cracking sound; this is normal. Massage the foot with your thumbs, fingers, or knuckles from top to bottom. Do one foot and then the other. It's easier if you cradle the foot in your lap. Be sensitive and gentle. Ask the person to tell you if any part hurts. Spend more time in places that are sore by gently pressing, rubbing, and massaging the area.

Always give a massage with your whole being—not just your hands. Be gentle, caring, and sensitive to what the other person is experiencing. A massage is an ideal way for two persons to become more in touch with their bodies and to release physical tension.

2.7 Leaving It at the River

My religion is kindness.
—Dalai Lama

Directions

1. Read the story of "Two Monks and the River."

Two Monks and the River

Two monks set out on their last day's journey to their monastery. At mid-morning they came upon a shallow river, and on the bank there stood a beautiful young maiden.

"May I help you cross?" asked the first monk.

"Why, yes, that would be most kind of you," replied the maiden.

So the first monk hoisted the maiden on his back and carried her across the river. They bowed and went their separate ways.

After an hour or two of walking, the second monk said to the first monk, "I can't believe you did that! I just can't believe it! We take vows of chastity, and you touched a woman. You even asked her! What are we going to tell the abbot when we get home? He's going to ask how our journey was, and we can't lie. What are we going to say?"

Another couple of hours passed and the second monk erupted again. "How could you do that? She didn't even ask. You offered! The abbot's going to be incredibly angry."

By late afternoon the two were nearing their home, and the second monk, now filled with anxiety, said, "I can't believe you did that! You touched a woman. You even carried her on your back. What are we going to tell the abbot?"

The first monk stopped, looked at the second monk, and said, "Listen, it's true that I carried that maiden across the river. But I left her at the river bank hours ago. You've been carrying her all day."

2. Which monk was the most stressed and why?

_____

_____

_____

3. Write a brief essay describing your interpretation of the story.

_____

_____

_____

_____

_____

_____

_____

_____

_____

_____

_____

4. When you are stressed or upset, what can you do to "leave it at the river"?

_____

_____

_____

_____

_____

_____

3.1 My Stressors

Never look down on somebody else unless you're helping them up.
—Jesse Jackson

Directions

1. Use the chart below to indicate the degree to which each item affects you.

2. For any frequent stressor, describe how it affects your life and offer strategies for lessening the frequency with which it occurs.

	Affects My Life		
Stressor	**Rarely/not at all**	**Sometimes**	**Frequently**
Academic			
Competition	_____	_____	_____
Schoolwork (difficult, low motivation)	_____	_____	_____
Exams and grades	_____	_____	_____
Poor resources (library, computers)	_____	_____	_____
Oral presentations/public speaking	_____	_____	_____
Professors/coaches (unfair, demanding, unavailable)	_____	_____	_____
Choosing and registering for classes	_____	_____	_____
Choosing a major/career	_____	_____	_____
Time			
Deadlines	_____	_____	_____
Procrastination	_____	_____	_____
Waiting for appointments and in lines	_____	_____	_____
No time to exercise	_____	_____	_____
Late for appointments or class	_____	_____	_____
Environment			
Others' behavior (rude, inconsiderate, sexist/racist)	_____	_____	_____
Injustice: seeing examples or being a victim of	_____	_____	_____
Crowds/large social groups	_____	_____	_____
Fears of violence/terrorism	_____	_____	_____
Weather (snow, heat/humidity, storms)	_____	_____	_____
Noise	_____	_____	_____
Lack of privacy	_____	_____	_____
Social			
Obligations, annoyances (family/friends/girl-/boyfriend)	_____	_____	_____
Not dating	_____	_____	_____
Roommate(s)/housemate(s) problems	_____	_____	_____
Concerns about STDs	_____	_____	_____

Stressor	Affects My Life		
	Rarely/not at all	Sometimes	Frequently
Self			
Behavior (habits, temper)	_____	_____	_____
Appearance (unattractive features, grooming)	_____	_____	_____
Ill health/physical symptoms	_____	_____	_____
Forgetting, misplacing, or losing things	_____	_____	_____
Weight/dietary management	_____	_____	_____
Self-confidence/self-esteem	_____	_____	_____
Boredom	_____	_____	_____
Money			
Not enough	_____	_____	_____
Bills/overspending	_____	_____	_____
Job: searching for or interviews	_____	_____	_____
Job/work issues (demanding; annoying)	_____	_____	_____
Tasks of Daily Living			
Tedious chores (shopping, cleaning)	_____	_____	_____
Traffic and parking problems	_____	_____	_____
Car problems (breakdowns, repairs)	_____	_____	_____
Housing (finding/getting or moving)	_____	_____	_____
Food (unappealing or unhealthful meals)	_____	_____	_____

3.2 My Stress Reactions

We know what we are, but know not what we may be.
—Shakespeare, *Hamlet*

Many people experience particular physical reactions to excessive stress. Here's a list of some common stress reactions. Which ones do you frequently experience? Can you add some reactions that are not on the list?

Reaction	Once a day	Once every 2–3 days	Once a week	Once a month	Not in the last 2 months
Headaches	_____	_____	_____	_____	_____
Nervous tics and twitches	_____	_____	_____	_____	_____
Blurred vision	_____	_____	_____	_____	_____
Dizziness	_____	_____	_____	_____	_____
Fatigue	_____	_____	_____	_____	_____
Coughing	_____	_____	_____	_____	_____
Wheezing	_____	_____	_____	_____	_____
Backache	_____	_____	_____	_____	_____
Muscle spasms	_____	_____	_____	_____	_____
Itching	_____	_____	_____	_____	_____
Excessive sweating	_____	_____	_____	_____	_____
Palpitations	_____	_____	_____	_____	_____
Constipation	_____	_____	_____	_____	_____
Jaw tightening	_____	_____	_____	_____	_____
Rapid heart rate	_____	_____	_____	_____	_____
Impotence	_____	_____	_____	_____	_____
Pelvic pain	_____	_____	_____	_____	_____
Stomachache	_____	_____	_____	_____	_____
Diarrhea	_____	_____	_____	_____	_____
Frequent urination	_____	_____	_____	_____	_____
Dermatitis (rash)	_____	_____	_____	_____	_____
Hyperventilation	_____	_____	_____	_____	_____
Irregular heart rhythm	_____	_____	_____	_____	_____
High blood pressure	_____	_____	_____	_____	_____
Delayed menstruation	_____	_____	_____	_____	_____
Vaginal discharge	_____	_____	_____	_____	_____
Nail biting	_____	_____	_____	_____	_____
Heartburn	_____	_____	_____	_____	_____

3.3 How Susceptible Am I to Stress?

Forget injuries, never forget kindnesses.
—Confucius

Some persons are more susceptible to the harmful effects of stress than others. The following inventory can give you an indication of your susceptibility. Score each item from 1 (almost always) to 5 (never) as it applies to you. A total score lower than 50 indicates you are not particularly vulnerable to stress. A score of 50 to 80 indicates moderate vulnerability, and a score of more than 80, high vulnerability—time to make some changes.

_____ 1. I eat at least one hot, nutritious meal a day.
_____ 2. I get 7 to 8 hours sleep at least four nights a week.
_____ 3. I am affectionate with others regularly.
_____ 4. I have at least one relative within 50 miles on whom I can rely.
_____ 5. I exercise to the point of sweating at least twice a week.
_____ 6. I smoke fewer than 10 cigarettes a day.
_____ 7. I drink fewer than five alcoholic drinks a week.
_____ 8. I am about the proper weight for my height and age.
_____ 9. I have enough money to meet basic expenses and needs.

_____ 10. I feel strengthened by my religious beliefs.
_____ 11. I attend club or social activities on a regular basis.
_____ 12. I have several close friends and acquaintances.
_____ 13. I have one or more friends to confide in about personal matters.
_____ 14. I am basically in good health.
_____ 15. I am able to speak openly about my feelings when angry or worried.
_____ 16. I discuss problems about chores, money, and daily living issues with the people I live with.
_____ 17. I do something just for fun at least once a week.
_____ 18. I am able to organize my time and do not feel pressured.
_____ 19. I drink fewer than three cups of coffee (or tea or cola drinks) a day.
_____ 20. I allow myself quiet time at least once during each day.

TOTAL
SCORE _____

Source: Adapted from a test developed by L. H. Miller, and A. D. Smith.

3.4 Warning Signs of Stress

Knock hard. Life is deaf.
—Mimi Parent

Do you have any of these warning signs of stress?

	No	Yes
Trouble falling asleep	_____	_____
Difficulty staying asleep	_____	_____
Waking up tired and not well rested	_____	_____
Fatigue	_____	_____
Changes in eating patterns	_____	_____
Craving sweet/fatty/salty foods ("comfort foods")	_____	_____
More headaches than usual	_____	_____
Short temper/irritable	_____	_____
Recurring colds and minor illness	_____	_____
Muscle ache or tightness	_____	_____
Trouble concentrating, remembering, or staying organized	_____	_____
Depression	_____	_____

3.5 My Life Changes and Stress

No bird flies too high if he flies with his own wings.
—William Blake

Directions

1. Mark any item in the Recent Life Changes Questionnaire (below) that has occurred in your life in the past one month.

2. Total the number of Life Change Units (LCUs) you have accumulated.

3. Refer to Chapter 3 of the text to determine if you are at risk for a health change.

Recent Life Changes Questionnaire

Life event	Life Change Units			Life Change Units	
	Women	Men		Women	Men
Death of son or daughter	135	103	Moderate illness	47	39
Death of spouse	122	113	Loss or damage of personal property	47	35
Death of brother or sister	111	87	Sexual difficulties	44	44
Death of parent	105	90	Getting demoted at work	44	39
Divorce	102	85	Major change in living conditions	44	37
Death of family member	96	78	Increase in income	43	30
Fired from work	85	69	Relationship problems	42	34
Separation from spouse due to marital problems	79	70	Trouble with in-laws	41	33
Major injury or illness	79	64	Beginning or ending school or college	40	35
Being held in jail	78	71	Making a major purchase	40	33
Pregnancy	74	55	New, close personal relationship	39	34
Miscarriage or abortion	74	51	Outstanding personal achievement	38	33
Death of a close friend	73	64	Troubles with coworkers at work	37	32
Laid off from work	73	59	Change in school or college	37	31
Birth of a child	71	56	Change in your work hours or conditions	36	32
Adopting a child	71	54	Troubles with workers whom you supervise	35	34
Major business adjustment	67	47	Getting a transfer at work	33	31
Decrease in income	66	49	Getting a promotion at work	33	29
Parents' divorce	63	52	Change in religious beliefs	31	27
A relative moving in with you	62	53	Christmas	30	25
Foreclosure on a mortgage or a loan	62	51	Having more responsibilities at work	29	29
Investment and/or credit difficulties	62	46	Troubles with your boss at work	29	29
Marital reconciliation	61	48	Major change in usual type or amount of recreation	29	28
Major change in health or behavior of family member	58	50	General work troubles	29	27
Change in arguments with spouse	55	41	Change in social activities	29	24
Retirement	54	48	Major change in eating habits	29	23
Major decision regarding your immediate future	54	46	Major change in sleeping habits	28	23
Separation from spouse due to work	53	54	Change in family get-togethers	28	20
An accident	53	38	Change in personal habits	27	24
Parental remarriage	52	45	Major dental work	27	23
Change residence to a different town, city, or state	52	39	Change of residence in same town or city	27	21
Change to a new type of work	51	50	Change in political beliefs	26	21
"Falling out" of a close personal relationship	50	41	Vacation	26	20
Marriage	50	50	Having fewer responsibilities at work	22	21
Spouse changes work	50	38	Making a moderate purchase	22	18
Child leaving home	48	38	Change in church activities	21	20
Birth of grandchild	48	34	Minor violation of the law	20	19
Engagement to marry	47	42	Correspondence course to help you in your work	19	16

Source: Adapted from Miller, M. A. and Rahe, R. H. (1997). Life changes scaling for the 1990s. *Journal of Psychosomatic Research, 43,* 279–292, with permission from Elsevier Science.

3.6 Prioritizing Tasks: First Things First

You must look into people as well as at them.
—Lord Chesterfield

Directions

1. Refer to your to-do list for today or create one for this exercise.

2. Sit or lie quietly for a few minutes to become mentally and physically relaxed (see note below).

3. Using a four-box chart, place each item on your to-do list in the appropriate box according to its *urgency* and *importance* (see example).

4. Carry out your tasks in this order: (1) urgent and important; (2) not urgent but important; (3) urgent but not important; and (4) not urgent and not important.

Note: Quieting yourself helps you distinguish the urgent/important tasks from the urgent/not important ones because urgency is a state of mind that makes tasks seem important even if they are not.

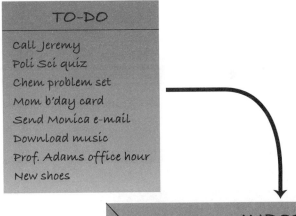

3.7 Time Audit for Time Management

*Half our life is spent trying to find something to do with the time we have
rushed through life trying to save.*

—Will Rogers

Directions

1. For three representative days in your life, keep a Time Diary (example
below) in which you record your activities for every hour of the day.
Make entries in your Time Diary two to three times a day. For
example, at noon, record your activities since awakening; at 5:00 P.M.
or so, record your activities since noon; at bedtime, record your
activities since 5:00 P.M.

Time	Activity
6:00 A.M.	wake up
6:15 A.M.	shower/dress/eat
7:00 A.M.	go to school
8:00 A.M.	Chem lecture
9:30 A.M.	hang out in library/snack
10:30 A.M.	Psych lecture
12:00 noon	job
5:00 P.M.	go home

2. Calculate the average daily hours and percentage of a day's time
spent in the following activities:

Time awake	_____hrs.	_____%
Time asleep	_____hrs.	_____%
Time traveling to and from work/school/activities	_____hrs.	_____%
Time spent at school	_____hrs.	_____%
Time spent studying/with schoolwork	_____hrs.	_____%
Time spent at job	_____hrs.	_____%
Time spent with family	_____hrs.	_____%
Time spent with friends	_____hrs.	_____%
Time spent with self	_____hrs.	_____%

3. Are you getting the recommended 7 to 8 hours of sleep per night? If
not, what could you change to get more sleep?

_____

_____

_____

_____

4. Can you identify windows of time that you can devote to priority
activities that now go neglected?

_____

_____

_____

_____

5. What did you learn from the Time Audit?

_____

_____

_____

_____

3.8 Are You a Procrastinator?

The journey of a thousand miles begins with the first step.
—Chinese proverb

Do you label yourself a procrastinator? Are you haunted by undone tasks? People who label themselves as procrastinators make the mistake of focusing on the end result of their activities (the end of the "journey of a thousand miles") instead of steps required to get to the end. Doing this can make getting to the end so difficult that they become stymied and put off moving toward their goal. And the more they put it off, the more formidable it seems because time is closing in. The way out of this is to focus on the first step instead of the end result.

Directions

1. Identify ONE task or goal that you cannot seem to do or move toward. Write it down here: _____.

2. Ask yourself, "What simple thing can I do today to move me toward my goal?" For example, if you are procrastinating about doing an assignment, take your textbook or lecture notes out of your backpack and make them visible. Write down here what step you could take: _____.

3. Do the step you wrote down in step 2.

4. When you are ready, ask yourself, "What step can I take now to move me toward my goal?" For example, you may decide to open your textbook or flip through your notes. Write it down here: _____

5. Do the step you wrote down in step 4.

6. Repeat steps 4 and 5 as many times as necessary to accomplish your goal. If all you can do is two steps, that's fine. At least you got started.

Note: Be alert for a voice in your head that tells you how lame you are for only doing a few steps or how lame this exercise is. This voice is trying to protect you from some harm it associates with accomplishing the goal. Sit quietly and "converse" with this voice (perhaps write out a dialogue) to lessen its effect on your behavior.

3.9 Image Visualization for Exam Anxiety

It ain't what we know that gives us trouble. It's what we know that ain't so that gives us trouble.

—Will Rogers

Because of school pressures and exam anxiety, students' health often suffers. Students suffer from tension and migraine headaches, stomach upsets, frequent infections, and a host of other mental and physical symptoms that are brought on or made worse by stress. Exam anxiety is learned behavior and it probably began quite early in your school life. (You may be able to recall the first time you experienced exam anxiety in school.) Like any learned behavior, exam anxiety can be unlearned or the response to it can be changed. There is absolutely nothing frightening or dangerous in exams themselves. Rather, the anxiety you experience is directly related to the importance you attach to your success on the exam. Obviously, if you feel that your whole life and future hinge on how well you score on an exam, you are constructing a situation that can cause severe anxiety and such physical symptoms as headaches and diarrhea.

Image visualization can be a powerful technique for reducing the panic and physical symptoms of exam anxiety. By using image visualization prior to an exam, you can teach your mind and body how to relax.

Directions

Step 1. Find a comfortable place in your house or apartment and a time when it is quiet. Pick an environment in which you feel secure and where there are no disturbing distractions. Sit in a comfortable chair or lie down on a couch, bed, or floor. The main thing is to get physically comfortable. If music helps you relax, you can play some of your favorite instrumental music, but it should not be so loud that it becomes intrusive.

Step 2. Close your eyes and ask your mind to recall a place where you felt content and happy. Let it be a place where you had the kind of positive feeling that you wish you had all the time. Use your imagination to reconstruct the scene or place where you felt comfortable and happy. It might be a vacation spot or a time when you were lying on a beach or hiking in the mountains. The main thing is to let your mind freely choose a place or memory that feels the most comfortable and to let yourself become totally involved in that scene. It's like having a daydream except that you are constructing your own dream. While your mind is engaged in this pleasurable memory, your body automatically relaxes.

Step 3. After your mind and body have become comfortable and relaxed, you can refocus your attention on an upcoming exam. You can visualize in your mind taking the exam while remaining relaxed and confident. Because your mind and body have already been relaxed and because you are secure and comfortable in your own environment, your mind will associate these positive feelings with the inner visualization of the exam. Use your imagination to project your mind into the future when you are taking the exam, being calm and confident as you write down the answers to the questions or write your essay.

Let your imagination construct all of the details of the exam situation. Visualize the exam room and where you are sitting; notice that you can read and understand the questions without any effort. Pay attention to how you feel as you take the exam and note the absence of anxiety and the absence of uncomfortable physical symptoms. Continue with the visualization until you feel comfortable with the experience and with the exam. Repeat this exercise for several days prior to the actual exam. When you take the exam you will be surprised at the absence of nervousness or anxiety; you will be even more surprised and pleased at the improvement in your grades.

4.1 Saying No

*Anyone can become angry. That is easy. But to be angry with the right person, to the right degree
at the right time, and for the right purpose—this is not easy.*

—Aristotle

Many people have a hard time saying *no* to the requests and demands made by others and an equally hard time saying *yes* to themselves for something they want. To be generous with time and energy is thought to be a virtue; to accommodate your own wishes, selfish. There are times, however, when saying *no* to others and *yes* to yourself is highly appropriate. Your emotions tell you those times. The time to say *no* is when saying *yes* makes you feel angry, stressed, resentful or unwell. The time to say *yes* to yourself is when it increases physical, emotional, and spiritual well-being.

Think about some recent times when you said *yes* to others when you really wanted to say *no.* Write them down like this: I would have liked to have said *no* when _____ asked me to _____.

Prepare yourself to say *no* to the same or other requests the next time they occur. Imagine yourself saying *no* to another and firmly and politely dealing with the other person's response.

Learning to say *no* may take practice, so don't get discouraged if at first you find it difficult.

4.2 My Definition of Mental Health

Success is getting up just one more time than you fall down.
—Barbara Milo Orbach

Directions

List and describe five characteristics of a mentally healthy person.

1. _____
   _____

2. _____
   _____
   _____

3. _____
   _____

4. _____
   _____

5. _____
   _____

If you were (are) a parent, how would you ensure that your child(ren) manifests the five characteristics on your list?

4.3 Keeping a Journal

As long as you derive inner help and comfort from anything, keep it.
—Mahatma Gandhi

Our emotions tell us how well we are fulfilling our life needs and how well we are achieving our life goals, but sometimes it is difficult to understand why we feel a certain way at a certain time. One way to clarify thoughts and feelings is to record them in a journal or notebook, which is something like a diary except that thoughts and feelings are recorded instead of specific events. Practice keeping a journal of your thoughts and feelings for a two-week period. Set aside a particular time each day, perhaps just before you go to sleep, to check in with your feelings by writing how you feel at that moment or how you felt that day and explaining why those feelings may have occurred.

- Use a special notebook for your journal.

- Write in a quiet place.

- Keep your journal private so you can be honest with yourself.

- Write continuously. Don't worry about grammar or spelling.

- Be expressive. Don't worry about making sense.

4.4 My Fears and Phobias

Those who flow as life flows know they need no other force. They feel no wear, they feel no tear; they need no mending, no repair.

—Lao Tzu

Many health behaviors are reflections of beliefs and attitudes that operate beneath the level of conscious awareness. Because these beliefs and attitudes in the mind are similar to programs in a computer, they *can* be changed. Your mind can create new, health-promoting programs to replace old, health-destroying ones.

Health problems often arise from destructive mental programs that have their origins in frightening life experiences, especially ones encountered early in life. If you can become aware of how such frightening experiences have programmed your mind and have thereby influenced your subsequent behavior, you can take steps to reprogram your mind and eliminate both the fear and the unwanted behavior.

Directions

Step 1. Identify your fears and phobias using the chart below.

Step 2. Sit or lie down in a quiet, comfortable place and allow your mind to recall experiences that may have caused one of your present fears—perhaps the one that bothers you the most. Allow yourself to relax your mind and body as much as possible, then let the images just freely enter your mind. When you encounter a frightening situation, *imagine* it taking place in a manner that is *not* frightening—in your mind, any scene can be changed so that you feel safe and comfortable. Let the situation resolve itself in a positive way. Remember, because everything is going on in your mind, you have complete control of all actions and events in your imagined scene.

Step 3. Practice this positive imagery until you feel that your fear is less intense.

Frightening Situations or objects	No fear	Mild fear	Strong fear
Airplanes	_____	_____	_____
Birds	_____	_____	_____
Bats	_____	_____	_____
Blood	_____	_____	_____
Cemeteries	_____	_____	_____
Dead animals	_____	_____	_____
Insects	_____	_____	_____
Crowds of people	_____	_____	_____
Dark places	_____	_____	_____
Dentists or doctors	_____	_____	_____
Hospitals	_____	_____	_____
Dirt or germs	_____	_____	_____
Lakes or oceans	_____	_____	_____
Dogs or cats	_____	_____	_____
Other animals	_____	_____	_____
Guns	_____	_____	_____
Closets or elevators	_____	_____	_____
Heights	_____	_____	_____
Public presentations	_____	_____	_____
Loud noises	_____	_____	_____
Driving in a car	_____	_____	_____
Being shouted at	_____	_____	_____
Being rejected	_____	_____	_____
Walking alone at night	_____	_____	_____
Other fears	_____	_____	_____

4.5 My Sleep and Dream Record

Life is what happens when you're making other plans.
—Tom Smothers

Each morning for one week, assess your sleep behavior with the aid of a chart like the one below. Also record the details of your dreams in a journal or notebook. Hints for dream recording:

1. Keep a pen or a pencil and a pad of paper near your bed.

2. Remind yourself before going to sleep that you want to remember your dreams.

3. Write down your dreams immediately upon awakening.

	Sun	Mon	Tues	Wed	Thurs	Fri	Sat
Time to bed							
Time fell asleep (estimate on waking)							
Feelings before falling asleep							
Trouble falling asleep? (yes or no)							
Take sleeping aid? (e.g., milk or pills)							
Number of times awake in the night							
Time woke up							
Time got out of bed							
Feelings on awakening							
Dreams? (yes or no)							
Total sleep time							

4.6 How Can I Sleep Better?

What lies behind us and what lies before us are tiny matters compared to what lies within us.
—Oliver Wendell Holmes

College students are notoriously poor sleepers. Which of the healthy sleep habits listed below could you incorporate into your life? Explain your reasoning.

- *Establish a regular sleep time.* Give your own natural sleep cycle a chance to be in synchrony with the day–night cycle by going to bed at the same time each night (within an hour more or less) and arising *without being awakened by an alarm clock.* This will mean going to bed early enough to give yourself enough time to sleep. Try to maintain your regular sleep times on the weekend. Getting up early during the week and sleeping late on weekends may upset the rhythm of your sleep cycle.

- *Create a proper (for you) sleep environment.* Sleep occurs best when the sleeping environment is dark, quiet, free of distractions, and not too warm. If you use radio or TV to help you fall asleep, use an autotimer to shut off the noise after falling asleep.

- *Wind down before going to bed.* About 20 to 30 minutes before bedtime, stop any activities that cause mental or physical arousal, such as work or exercise, and take up a "quiet" activity that can create a transition to sleep. Transitional activities could include reading, watching "mindless" TV, taking a warm bath or shower, meditation, or making love.

- *Make the bedroom for sleeping only.* Make the bedroom your place for getting a good night's sleep. Try not to use it for work or for discussing problems with your partner.

- *Don't worry while in bed.* If you are unable to sleep after about 30 minutes in bed because of worry about the next day's activities, get up and do some limited activity such as reading a magazine article, doing the dishes, or meditating. Go back to bed when you feel drowsy. If you cannot sleep because of thinking about all that you have to do, write down what's on your mind and let the paper hold onto the thoughts while you sleep. You can retrieve them in the morning.

- *Avoid alcohol and caffeine.* Some people have a glass of beer or wine before bed to relax. Large amounts of alcohol, although sedating, block normal sleep and dreaming patterns. Because caffeine remains in the body for several hours, people sensitive to caffeine should not ingest any after noon.

- *Exercise regularly.* Exercising 20 to 30 minutes three or four times a week enhances the ability to sleep. You should not exercise vigorously within three hours of bedtime, however, because of the possibility of becoming too aroused to sleep.

4.7 How Do I Affect Others?

My granary has burned down—now I can see the sun.
—Japanese proverb

You can influence how others feel simply by your words and actions. When you sincerely say to someone, "You look terrific," you make that person feel good, thereby initiating a series of psychophysiological processes that begin in the mind and affect hormonal and nervous regulation of the body in such a way that his or her wellness is enhanced. On the other hand, when you say to someone, "You look terrible," you can initiate physiological responses that are correspondingly negative.

Directions

Step 1. For one week keep a record of the remarks you make to others that may affect their health and well-being, either positively or negatively. For example:

To John: "I liked the way you handled your anger in that situation. How'd you do it?"
To Sue (who is overweight): "You sure do pack away the food. I don't see where you put it all."

Step 2. For one week try to avoid remarks that can hurt a person's feelings or make a person feel bad. Say positive things to the people you interact with. Tell others how well they look and how well they are doing things. Show them that you care how they feel. As people around you feel better, so will you.

5.1 My Estimated Daily Calorie Requirement

There are two ways of being disappointed in life; one is not to get what you want and the other is to get it.
—George Bernard Shaw

Estimate your daily calorie requirement using steps 1–4 below.

Step 1. I am _____feet _____ inches tall.

Step 2. Calculate your total body mass units:

• Women: Allow 100 body mass units for the first 5 feet of height + 5 body mass units for each additional inch.

• Men: Allow 106 body mass units for the first 5 feet of height + 6 body mass units for each additional inch.

My total body mass units = _____.

Step 3. My activity factor is:

Sedentary = 13
Active = 15
Very active = 17

Step 4. Calculate your estimated daily calories by multiplying your body mass units by your activity factor:

(Body mass units) × (Activity factor) = _____ (my estimated calories)

5.2 My Food Diary

If your stomach disputes you, lay down and pacify it with cool thoughts.
—Leroy "Satchel" Paige

Directions

For two days that are representative of your usual food consumption patterns, keep a list of *everything* you eat (see illustration below). Record:

- the name of each food item

- the quantity of each food item consumed

- the time of day each item was consumed

- whether consumption was part of a meal or as a snack

- whether you ate because of hunger or for other reasons

- your feelings at the time you ate

- the social circumstances surrounding eating (alone, with friends, with family, etc.)

Food	Quantity	Time of day	Meal or snack	Hungry? Other?	Feelings?	Social?
cereal	bowlful	6:30 AM	meal	hungry	sleepy	alone
banana	one					
milk, skim	cup					

Data Analysis

1. How close are you to the recommended Five-A-Day servings of fruits and vegetables?

   _____

   _____

   _____

   _____

2. Describe your snacking patterns.

   _____

   _____

   _____

   _____

3. Describe ways your feelings affect your food consumption.

   _____

4. Log on to the U.S. Department of Agriculture's nutritional analysis Web site (http://www.mypyramid.gov).

   - Click the My Pyramid Plan link and enter the appropriate data for your age, sex, and level of physical activity to determine your nutritional recommendations. Print the response.

   - On the Web page with your recommendations, click the Meal Tracking Worksheet link and analyze your diet by filling in the spreadsheet.

5.3 My Dietary Analysis

People are satisfied, not by the presence of food, but by the absence of greed.
—Gurdjieff

Refer to your Food Diary and consult the U.S. Department of Agriculture's MyPyramid Web site (http://www.mypyramid.gov) to analyze the nutrient content of your diet and to obtain recommendations for improving the nutrient quality of your diet.

Directions

1. Log on to MyPyramid.gov

2. Click the My Pyramid Plan link and enter the appropriate data for your age, sex, and level of physical activity to determine your nutritional recommendations. Print the response.

3. On the Web page with your recommendations, click the MyPyramid Tracker link and enter the foods from your Food Diary for a day that is typical of your dietary pattern.

4. Click the Analyze Your Food Intake tab and obtain an analysis of your diet and recommendations for a healthy diet by clicking (and printing out):

    • Meeting 2005 Dietary Guidelines

    • Nutrient Intakes

    • MyPyramid Recommendations

4. On a typical day, I consume:

    _____ grams of fiber
    _____ grams of total fat
    _____ grams of saturated fat
    _____ grams of cholesterol
    _____ milligrams of calcium
    _____ milligrams of iron
    _____ grams of sodium

5. How does your diet compare to the MyPyramid recommendations?

    _____

    _____

    _____

    _____

    _____

    _____

    _____

    _____

    _____

    _____

5.4 Fast-Food Restaurant Research

After dinner sit awhile. After supper walk a mile.
—English proverb

Each day approximately 20% of the U.S. population eats at a fast-food restaurant. The reasons for patronizing such establishments are convenience (they are everywhere), perceived lack of time to shop and prepare meals at home, fast food's taste and texture, the need to mollify nagging children, and cost. Since fast food is so popular and prevalent, it is healthful to know the nutrient content of the fast food you consume. So . . .

Directions

1. Go to your favorite fast-food restaurant and ask the serviceperson for a copy of the brochure listing the nutritional content of that establishment's foods. (If you do not patronize such establishments, do the assignment for someone you know who does and share the information with her or him.)

2. Choose a fast-food meal that is typical for you. Refer to the restaurant's brochure, and for each of the meal's components list the following information:
   - Total calories
   - Grams of protein
   - Total grams of fat
   - Total grams of saturated fat
   - mg of cholesterol
   - mg of salt
   - Grams of fiber

3. Calculate the dollar cost of the energy content of the meal (divide total calories by the total cost). This tells you how much bang (energy) you are getting for your buck.

4. What percentage of your estimated daily calories is contributed by this meal?

   _____

   _____

5. Describe your experience obtaining the company's brochure at the restaurant.

   _____

   _____

6. List the reasons you patronize this establishment.

   _____

   _____

7. How frequently do you patronize fast-food restaurants?

   _____

   _____

8. What did you learn from this assignment?

   _____

   _____

Note: Fast Food Facts (http://www.foodfacts.info) lists the nutrient composition of fast foods. Most fast-food corporations list nutrient composition of their products on the company Web site. Whereas it is possible to analyze the data for this assignment with that Web tool, it is more interesting and makes you a better health consumer if you go personally to the restaurant and ask for the data.

5.5 Can I Read a Food Label?

*If more of us valued food and cheer and song above hoarded gold, it would
be a merrier world.*
—J. R. R. Tolkien

Directions

1. Look at the Nutrition Facts Label on any commercial food product. The Percent Daily Values says that a person with a 2,000 calories per day energy requirement should not ingest more than how many grams of fat per day?

   _____

   _____

2. How many milligrams of cholesterol per day are recommended for someone with a daily calorie requirement of 2,000 calories? 2,500 calories?

   _____

   _____

3. Take the Food Label Quiz at the U.S. Food and Drug Administration's Center for Food Safety and Applied Nutrition Web site: http://www.cfsan.fda.gov/~dms/flquiz1.html. Find out the following information:

- Which muffins maximize fiber intake?

  _____

  _____

  _____

- Are these pretzels low in sodium?

  _____

- Which has less calories, the low-fat blueberry yogurt or the low-fat cherry yogurt?

  _____

  _____

- Which is the best source of calcium?

  _____

  _____

- Which packaged food has the least saturated fat?

  _____

  _____

6.1 My Body Weight

People through finding something beautiful, think something else unbeautiful. Through finding one man fit, judge another unfit.

—Lao Tzu

My height in feet and inches (without shoes):_____

My weight in pounds now (with clothes):_____

My highest weight as an adult = _____ pounds, which I weighed when I was _____ years old

My lowest weight as an adult = _____ pounds, which I weighed when I was _____ years old

The recommended weight for my height and body frame is (see text Chapter 6):_____

My body mass index* is _____.
(See the chart on text page 135 or the online calculator at (http://nhlbisupport.com/bmi/.)

The circumference of my body at my waist[†] is _____.
The circumference of my body at my hips is _____.
The ratio[‡] of my waist/hip circumferences is _____.

---

*The Body Mass Index (BMI) is the most common way doctors assess the relationship of body size and health. It is calculated by dividing a person's weight in kilograms by her or his height in meters squared: BMI = wgt/(hgt)(hgt). A BMI between 18 and 24.9 is not associated with an increased risk of weight-related illness. (*Note:* The health risks for a BMI over 25 are less reliable for people who are muscular or of a large body frame.)

[†]A waist circumference of more than 40 inches in men and 35 inches in women indicates overweight.

[‡]A waist-to-hip ratio of 0.95 in men and 0.80 in women indicates overweight.

6.2 My Body Image

Hope for the best, plan for the worst.
　　　　　　　—Chinese proverb

Body image (more accurately, *body esteem*) is a self-appraisal of your body's size and shape.

Directions:

1. Do the Body Image questionnaire below.
    How do you feel about the appearances of these regions of your body?

    _____

    _____

	Quite satisfied	Somewhat satisfied	Somewhat dissatisfied	Very dissatisfied
Hair	❏	❏	❏	❏
Arms	❏	❏	❏	❏
Hands	❏	❏	❏	❏
Feet	❏	❏	❏	❏
Waist	❏	❏	❏	❏
Buttocks	❏	❏	❏	❏
Hips	❏	❏	❏	❏
Legs and ankles	❏	❏	❏	❏
Thighs	❏	❏	❏	❏
Chest or breasts	❏	❏	❏	❏
Posture	❏	❏	❏	❏
General attractiveness	❏	❏	❏	❏

2. Write an essay in which you respond to these questions:

    *   Which of your regular thoughts and actions are likely to enhance your body image?

        _____

        _____

    *   Which of your regular thoughts and actions are likely to be detrimental to your body image?

        _____

        _____

    *   How do social expectations of body size and shape affect your body image?

        _____

        _____

    *   How susceptible are you to media images of "ideal" body proportions for members of your sex?

        _____

        _____

    *   How could you become more satisfied with your body image?

        _____

        _____

        _____

7.1 My Target Heart Rate Zone

You should ask yourself every day why you are doing what you're doing.
—Robert Arneson

Your target heart rate zone is the level of activity that leads to maximum conditioning. Activity below the target heart rate zone conditions little; activity above the target heart rate zone may be dangerous for some people.

The pattern of the preferred exercise session is shown in the following figure:

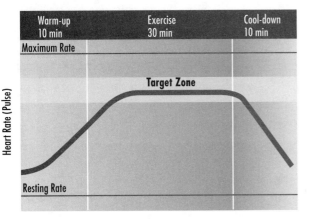

To compute your target heart rate zone:

1. Subtract your age from 220 (Example: For a 20-year-old person with resting heart rate of 80 beats/min: $220 - 20 = 200$).

2. Subtract resting heart rate from number obtained in step 1 ($200 - 80 = 120$).

3. Multiply the result once by 0.65 and once again by 0.75 ($120 \times .65 = 78; 120 \times .75 = 90$).

4. Add resting heart rate to the results obtained in step 3 to give lower and upper heart rates of target zone (Lower limit: $78 + 80 = 158$; upper limit: $90 + 80 = 170$).

After your warm-up period and 10 minutes of activity, take your pulse and compare it to the heart rate for your target zone level of activity. If you are below your target zone heart rate, increase your activity. If above, slow down.

Measuring Heart Rate

Your heart rate, or pulse, is the number of times your heart beats per minute. When your heart beats, it pushes about a cup of blood into your circulatory system. At certain sites in the circulatory system you can feel when the blood from the most recent heartbeat arrives. These sites are where you measure your heart rate. The most commonly used are in the neck (carotid artery), the wrist below the thumb (radial artery), or the inner thigh (femoral artery). To measure your heart rate:

- Get a clock/watch that measures seconds.

- Place your first two fingers, not your thumb (it has a pulse and can confuse things), on one of the common measuring sites (neck, wrist, or inner thigh).

- Press a tiny bit to make solid contact with the tissue under the skin (including the artery).

- Move your fingers around until the sensation of the pulse is strongest.

- Look at your timing device and count the number of beats/pulsations in 15 seconds.

- Multiply the number of beats/pulsations in 15 seconds by 4 to get beats per minute.

7.2 My Fitness Index

People measure their esteem of each other by what each has and not by what each is. . . . Nothing can bring you peace but yourself.
—Ralph Waldo Emerson

The Harvard Step Test is a standardized measure of cardiorespiratory fitness. To carry out the Harvard Step Test, you need to be comfortably dressed (athletic clothes are best); you need a chair, stool, or bench 12–18 inches high, a stopwatch or clock with a second hand, a pencil and paper, and a metronome or some other method to produce a rhythmic 100–120 beats per minute, such as a recording of a march or some disco music. Once all this is assembled, you can begin.

1. Make a 15-second recording of your resting pulse and multiply by 4 to obtain your rate per minute.

2. Start the metronome or music; 120 beats per minute.

3. Step completely up on the bench with the left leg first, followed by your right leg, then step back down with the left leg first, followed by the right. The stepping should be done on a four-count: up-up-down-down; up-up-down-down. . . .

4. Continue the exercise for 3 minutes unless you are more than 30 years old and have been rather inactive for more than six months. In that case, do the test for only a minute or two, whichever you think you can do. If you are sure you cannot do the test for even a few seconds, don't.

5. When the 3 minutes of exercise are through, immediately take your pulse. Record the number of heartbeats between 15 and 30 seconds after exercising. Make another heart rate measurement between 60 and 75 seconds; another between 120 and 135 seconds; another between 180 and 195 seconds; another between 240 and 255 seconds; and a final measurement between 300 and 315 seconds.

6. Multiply each of the 15-second heart rates by 4 to give the beats per minute. Record your data on the graph provided.

7. Compute your Fitness Index: Add the per-minute heart rates for the first 3 minutes after exercise. Then divide that number into 30,000.

Fitness index	Rating
above 90	Excellent
80–89	Good
65–79	Average
55–64	Low Average
below 55	Poor

Harvard Step Test Data Record

Time	Heartbeats per 15 Seconds	Heartbeats per Minute
At rest	_____ × 4 =	_____
15–30 sec.	_____ × 4 =	_____
60–75 sec.	_____ × 4 =	_____
120–135 sec.	_____ × 4 =	_____
180–195 sec.	_____ × 4 =	_____
240–255 sec.	_____ × 4 =	_____
300–315 sec.	_____ × 4 =	_____

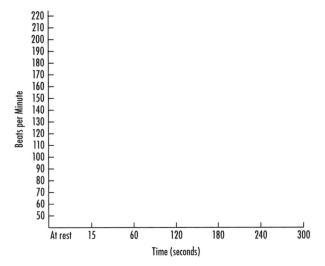

7.3 My Flexibility Index

You don't have to learn the lotus position or climb to the top of a mountain in Tibet to be able to sit down and relax your mind.
—College health student

Body flexibility is a fundamental aspect of feeling good and keeping your body healthy. Use this simple YMCA test to determine your degree of body flexibility, and continue to use it to determine your progress in becoming more limber.

1. Warm up with some stretching before the test.

2. Sit on the floor with your legs extended and feet a few inches apart.

3. With a piece of adhesive tape, mark the place where your heels touch the floor. Your heels should touch the near edge of the tape.

4. Place a yardstick on the floor between your legs and parallel to them. The beginning of the yardstick should be closest to you and the 15-inch mark should align with the near edge of the tape.

5. Slowly reach with both hands as far forward as possible. Touch your fingers to the yardstick to determine the distance reached. Do not jerk to increase your distance—this may cause damage to your leg muscles.

6. Repeat the exercise two or three times and record your best score.

	Inches reached		Rating
Men	Women		
22–23	24–27		Excellent
20–21	21–23		Good
14–19	16–20		Average
12–13	13–16		Fair
0–11	0–12		Poor

7.4 The Sun Salute

The best way to avoid something is to cause that which is to be avoided to avoid you of its own accord.
—Sufi saying

The sun salute, a Hatha yoga exercise, is a series of 12 postures, or asanas, intended to be done in one flowing routine. Each of the 12 postures is held for 3 seconds. The entire routine should be done at least twice in succession, alternating the legs. The Sun Salute is an excellent way to stretch the body every morning or any time you may need to relax tense muscles and restore deep, regular breathing. Try it.

Position 1 Stand erect with your feet hip-width apart and palms together in front of your chest. Inhale and exhale slowly and calmly.

Position 2 Inhaling, raise your arms above your head, palms facing in. Lengthen through the spine, but do not arch your back.

Position 3 Exhaling, bend forward from the hips, keeping your arms extended and your head hanging loosely between them. Keep your legs slightly bent and relax your neck and shoulders.

Position 4 Inhaling, bend both knees and place your palms flat an the floor by the outsides of your feet. Extend your left leg back. Stretch your chin toward the ceiling.

Position 5 Continue while holding the breath if you can—don't strain. Reach your forward leg back next to the other leg. Hold your body straight, supported by your hands and toes, with ankles, hips, and shoulders in a straight plane.

Position 6 Exhaling, lower your knees, chest, and chin or forehead to the floor, keeping your hips up and toes curled under.

Position 7 Inhaling, bring the tops of your feet to the floor, straighten your legs, and come up to straight arms, opening the chest and stretching your chin toward the ceiling. Be careful not to overarch your lower back.

Position 8 Exhaling, curl your toes under and raise your hips into an inverted "V." Push back with your hands and lengthen your spine by reaching your hips upward. Keep your head hanging loosely.

Position 9 Inhaling, lift your head and bring your left leg between your hands, keeping the right leg back. Raise your chin toward the ceiling.

Position 10 Exhaling, bring your left foot forward so your feet are together. Bend forward from the hips, keeping your legs slightly bent and your upper body relaxed. If you can, touch your head to your knees and place your palms beside your feet.

Position 11 Inhaling, slowly straighten up with your arms extended above your head. If you have any lower back pain, be sure to bend your knees.

Position 12 Exhaling, bring your hands together in front of you. Close your eyes for a moment and feel the sensations in your body.

8.1 Sexual Anatomy

You cannot live a perfect day without doing something for someone who will never be able to repay you.
—Coach John Wooden

Directions

On the following pages are silhouettes of the male and female pelvic regions and a page of drawings of the sexual/reproductive organs. Cut out the organs and attach them to the proper positions on the silhouettes found on pages 95–97, and label the female front view on page 98.

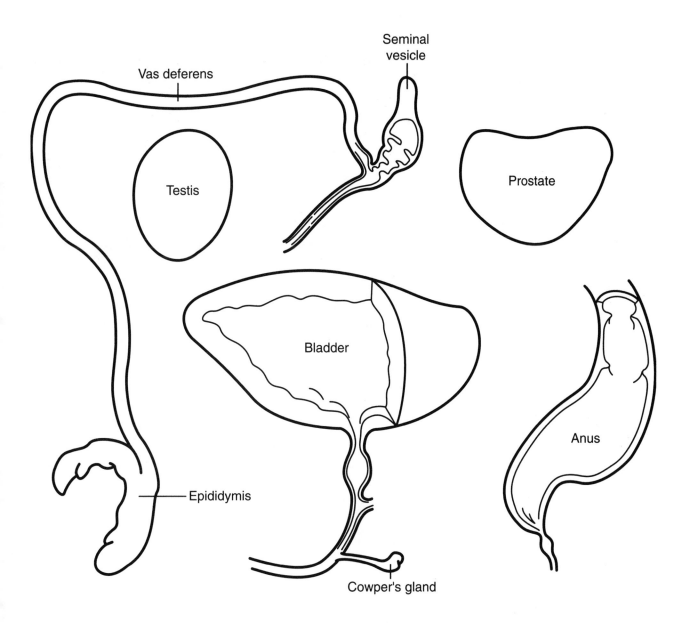

Male side

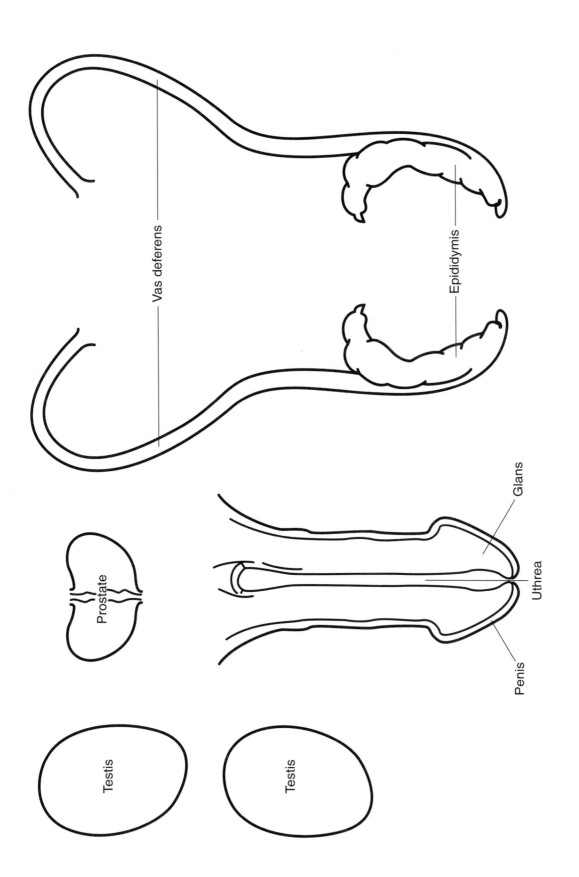

Male front

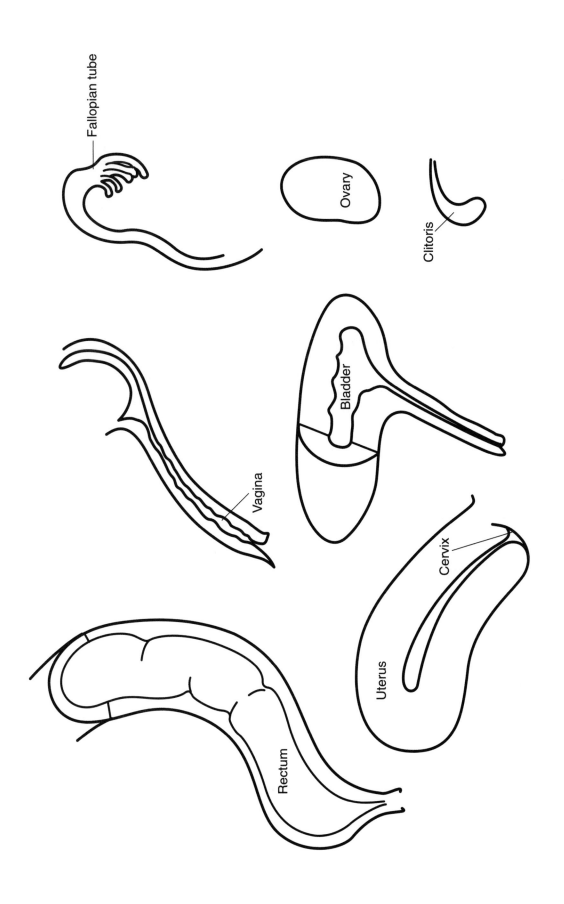

Fallopian tube

Ovary

Clitoris

Bladder

Vagina

Cervix

Uterus

Rectum

Female side

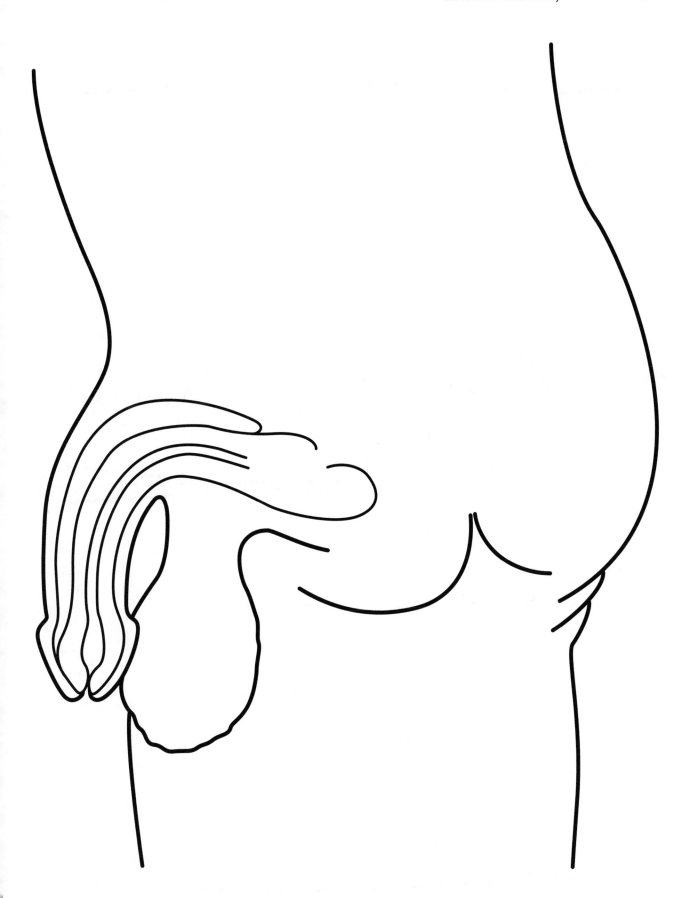

Male side

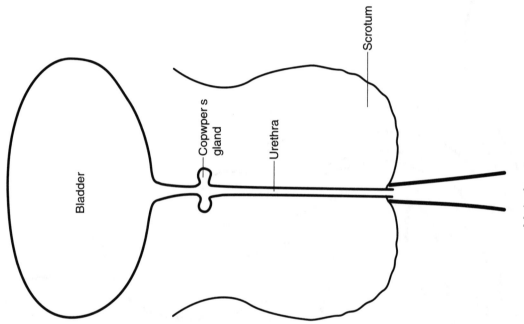

Bladder

Copwper s gland

Urethra

Scrotum

Male front

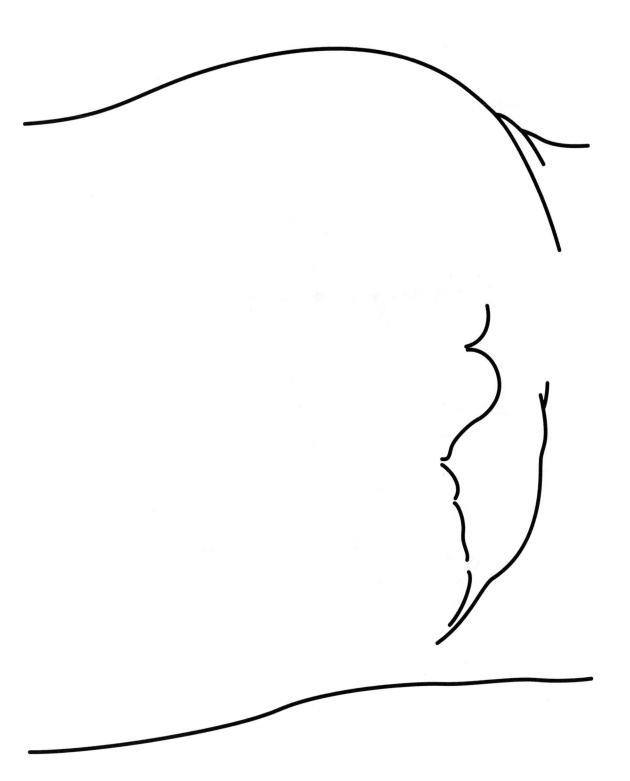

Female side

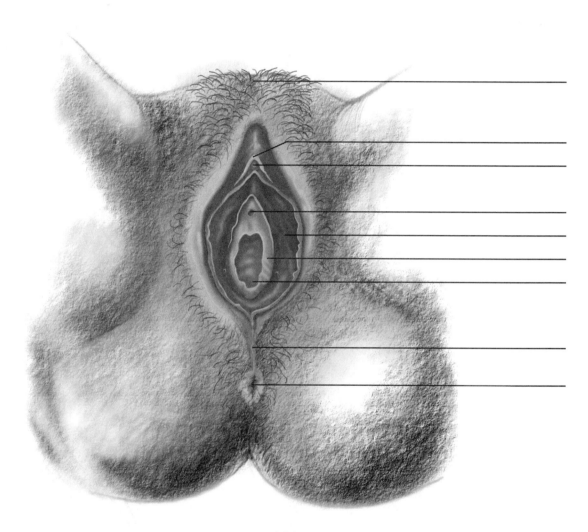

Label

1. Anus
2. Clitoris
3. Labia majora
4. Labia minora
5. Mons veneris
6. Perineum
7. Prepuce (hood)
8. Urinary meatus
9. Vaginal orifice

8.2 My Sexual Attitudes

Steer clear of the front of a billygoat, the back of a horse, and all sides of a fool.

—Yiddish proverb

Write a one-paragraph response to the following questions. Your responses will be read only by the instructor and will be kept strictly confidential.

1. Describe how your current sexual attitudes and beliefs compare to those of your parents (give examples).

   _____

   _____

   _____

   _____

   _____

2. Describe the ways religious/spiritual values affect your sexuality and sexual behavior.

   _____

   _____

   _____

   _____

   _____

3. What is the importance of sex in human relationships?

   _____

   _____

   _____

   _____

   _____

4. By what criteria, if any, is sexual intercourse before marriage permissible? How would you advise your own child on having premarital sex?

   _____

   _____

   _____

   _____

5. Describe two social expectations of you as a member of your sex.

   _____

   _____

   _____

   _____

   _____

   Complete the following statements based upon your experiences and thoughts.

6. When I was growing up, talking about sexual matters with my parents . . .

   _____

   _____

   _____

   _____

7. As a child and teenager I learned the most about sex from . . .

   _____

   _____

   _____

   _____

8. The way I reacted to how my body changed at puberty was . . . especially . . .

   _____

   _____

   _____

   _____

9. My first significant sexual experience (not necessarily intercourse) taught me that . . .

   _____

   _____

   _____

   _____

10. From my parents' marriage I learned . . .

   _____

   _____

   _____

   _____

8.3 My Sexual Values

We do not see things as they are. We see things as we are.
—Talmud

For each statement, indicate the response that most closely identifies your beliefs and attitudes. Use the following code:

A = I strongly agree   B = I slightly agree

C = I slightly disagree   D = I strongly disagree

_____ 1. Men are by nature more sexually aggressive than women are and enjoy sex more than women do.

_____ 2. Sex-role definitions and stereotypes get in the way of mutually satisfying sexual relations.

_____ 3. Concern over sexual performance is quite common.

_____ 4. Psychologically healthy people don't experience any guilt over their sexual activities.

_____ 5. If a woman doesn't experience orgasm, it is generally because the man has not been sensitive enough to her needs.

_____ 6. If a man experiences erection problems, it is generally because of the woman's lack of appreciation of his manhood.

_____ 7. In a sexual relationship, it is the job of each partner to make the other feel like a woman or a man.

_____ 8. Getting in touch with our sexual attractions and feelings toward others generally leads to overt sexual behavior.

_____ 9. The quality of a sexual relationship is usually parallel to the quality of the partners' relationship in general.

_____ 10. Sexual freedom implies doing whatever consenting adults agree to.

_____ 11. If we want to, we can reeducate ourselves so that we can experience sexual relationships with numerous partners without feeling guilty.

_____ 12. Sexual freedom ought to be counterbalanced by sexual responsibility.

_____ 13. We will probably be no more sexually attractive to others than we are to ourselves.

_____ 14. Discussing sexual wants and needs generally leads to mechanical and unspontaneous sex.

_____ 15. Extramarital sex inevitably causes dissatisfaction in the marital relationships.

_____ 16. Today's generation is really unconcerned about being sexually inadequate.

_____ 17. Most people who are intimate with each other find it relatively easy to talk openly and honestly about the intimate details of sexuality.

_____ 18. The key to improving sexual satisfaction is to master sexual techniques and skills.

_____ 19. Sex without love is unsatisfying.

8.4 Sexual Communication

If the person you are talking to doesn't appear to be listening, be patient. It may simply be that he has a piece of fluff in his ears.
—A. A. Milne, Winnie-the-Pooh

Communication skills contribute to rewarding relationships in many ways. Many of the problems couples experience could be avoided or easily resolved with more effective communication skills. How are your communication skills?

For each statement, circle the appropriate number of points.

	Usually	Sometimes	Seldom
1. I find it easy to express my nonsexual needs and feelings to others.	2	1	0
2. I find it easy to express my sexual needs and feelings to others.	2	1	0
3. I am sensitive to the needs and feelings expressed by others, and especially their nonverbal expressions.	2	1	0
4. My relationships with other people are pleasant and rewarding.	2	1	0
5. When a conflict arises in one of my relationships, it is resolved with ease.	2	1	0
6. I find it easy to communicate with people of both genders.	2	1	0
7. I can communicate effectively with people of various ethnic groups.	2	1	0
8. I can find the right words to express the ideas I want to convey.	2	1	0
9. I am good at interpreting nonverbal messages from other people.	2	1	0
10. I try very hard not to interrupt someone who is speaking to me.	2	1	0
11. I try very hard to be nonjudgmental in my responses when people share their ideas and feelings with me.	2	1	0
12. When a discussion is causing me to feel uncomfortable, I try hard not to withdraw from the discussion or change the subject.	2	1	0
13. I try to help people open up by asking open-ended, rather than yes-or-no questions.	2	1	0
14. When I want to express my feelings, I try to phrase them as "I" statements, rather than "you" statements.	2	1	0
15. I feel that I am adequately assertive.	2	1	0
16. I let someone know when they are not respecting my rights or feelings.	2	1	0
17. I find it easy to say no to pressure for unwanted sexual activity.	2	1	0
18. I find it easy to talk to a potential sexual partner about prevention of sexually transmitted diseases.	2	1	0
19. When conflicts arise in my relationships, I am, if necessary, willing and able to make a compromise to resolve the conflict.	2	1	0
20. When conflicts arise in my relationships, I try to find a resolution that satisfies the needs of both persons involved.	2	1	0

TOTAL POINTS:_____

Interpretation:

36 to 40 points: You have developed highly effective patterns of communication and assertiveness.

32 to 35 points: You have above-average communication and assertiveness skills.

28 to 31 points: You have about-average communication and assertiveness skills. Sharpening these skills will improve your relationships and need fulfillment.

27 points or less: It would be very rewarding for you to improve your communication skills. Your relationships would function much better, and you would experience much greater need fulfillment.

Source: Byer, C. O., Shainberg, L. W., & Galliano, G. (1999). *Dimensions of human sexuality.* Boston, MA: McGraw-Hill College, p. 68.

8.5 My Attitudes About Love

We must always follow somebody looking for truth, and we must always run away from anyone who finds it.
—Andre Gide

Directions

For each of the following statements, circle the number that most closely approximates your response.

	Strongly agree	Somewhat agree	Strongly disagree
1. I don't believe that research should be done on love, because love should remain mysterious.	3	2	1
2. Love is the most important thing in my life.	3	2	1
3. My life is very unhappy when I am not in love.	3	2	1
4. I am able to function very well without someone to love.	1	2	3
5. Love is a fantasy that is popular with 13-year-old girls.	1	2	3
6. Each of us has our "one and only" somewhere out there, if only we can find that person.	3	2	1
7. Once you find your "one and only," you will never feel attracted to anyone else.	3	2	1
8. If you love too much, you will only get hurt.	1	2	3
9. I am able to function very well without someone loving me.	1	2	3
10. The smartest people don't get hung up on someone.	1	2	3
11. You can tell when you first see someone if you are going to love that person.	3	2	1
12. The best relationships have some basis more important than love.	1	2	3
13. If you love someone enough, any kind of problem in the relationship can be overcome.	3	2	1
14. If I had to choose between living in poverty or living without love, I would choose to love in poverty.	3	2	1
15. As soon as someone thinks you love them, that person will start to take advantage of you.	1	2	3
16. You're a sucker if you fall in love with someone who has no money.	1	2	3

TOTAL POINTS: _____

Interpretation:

40 to 48 points: You have very romantic ideas about love. You might put too much emphasis on love as a basis for a partnership, while ignoring other important considerations.

24 to 39 points: You have more realistic ideas about love. Love is important to you, but you also are aware of the many other bases of a smoothly functioning partnership.

16 to 23 points: You appear to be pretty cynical about love. Maybe you previously have been hurt or come from a family where romance was not emphasized. Your attitudes might insulate you from getting hurt again but could also be preventing you from enjoying the benefits of a loving relationship.

Source: Byer, C. O., Shainberg, L. W., & Galliano, G. (1999). *Dimensions of human sexuality.* Boston, MA: McGraw-Hill College, p. 86.

8.6 My Relationship Wants and Needs

A second touching a hot stove seems like an hour. An hour touching a pretty
girl seems like a second. Now that's relativity.
—Albert Einstein

Directions

1. What are your wants and needs in a love relationship? Choose the three most important items from the list below.

   _____

   _____

   _____

2. Consider the list again and choose the singlemost important item.

   _____

3. Write your choices and the reasons for choosing them.

   _____

   _____

   _____

4. Optional: Which items does your partner choose?

   _____

I want someone to . . .

Love me
Confide in me
Show me affection
Respect my needs
Appreciate what I wish to achieve
Understand my moods
Help me make important decisions
Stimulate my ambition
Look up to
Give me self-confidence
Stand by me in difficulty
Appreciate me as I am
Admire my ability
Make me feel that I count for something
Relieve my loneliness
Support me and our children
Accept my need to be self-sufficient and independent

8.7 My Relationship Values

Love is many things, but more than anything it is a disturbance of the digestive system.
—Gabriel Garcia Marquez, February 14, 1995

What are your priorities in a love relationship? Rate the items in the list below with a number from 1 to 10, using 1 to indicate least importance to you and 10 most importance to you.

Write in a one-page essay in which you describe the three items you feel most strongly about and why.

_____ Being able to talk comfortably to my partner about my innermost feelings

_____ Having my partner share with me his/her innermost feelings

_____ Sharing with my partner nearly all of my leisure time

_____ Both of us having similar political beliefs

_____ Each of us having our own careers

_____ Being able to express anger to my partner

_____ Having my partner express his/her anger to me

_____ Being able to have sexual relations with other people

_____ Having good relations with my parents and family

_____ Enjoying what we have now without concern for a lifelong relationship

_____ Having mutual close friends

_____ Having similar religious beliefs

_____ Having major interests and friendships of my own outside the relationship

_____ Wanting the same material possessions (house, car, etc.)

_____ Being able to tell my partner when I feel jealous

_____ Having the most influence over how we as a couple spend money

_____ Trying with my partner new sexual experiences and techniques

_____ Working together on tasks rather than dividing them between us

_____ Having children

8.8 Listening Exercise

*One of the lessons of history is that nothing is sometimes a good thing to do,
and often a clever thing to say.*
—Will Durant

Directions

Ask someone to be the speaker for this exercise. Carry out steps 1–4 below.
So that you can observe body language (very important for discerning the
speaker's emotions), do the assignment in person, not on the phone or via
e-mail or IM, or text messaging.

Step 1. Topic 1: Ask the speaker to tell you something that's important
to her or him. The first time you do this it's better that the topic *not*
involve you personally or your relationship with the speaker. Let the
speaker talk for up to five minutes.

Step 2. While the speaker is talking, *just listen,* and notice any urges you
have to stop paying attention or to interrupt with suggestions or
comments. Notice where your attention goes, for example, if your
mind drifts to other topics or you daydream. Notice if you feel critical
or if you have the urge to comment or advise.

Step 3. When the speaker has finished, tell her or him what you
experienced. Share with the speaker if you were able to pay full
attention to what was being said or if your mind was busy with
something else. If you're new at this, you'll probably notice that it's
difficult simply to listen.

Step 4. Topic 2: Do the exercise a second time. Ask the speaker to
address a topic different from that addressed in step 1. Also, instead
of telling the speaker your experience with listening, tell the speaker
a paraphrase of what she or he said using

- an *emotion word* that describes the speaker's feelings (not yours!)
- a *because statement* that describes the reason for that emotion
  from the speaker's point of view (not yours!)

As a noun, the word *paraphrase* means a condensed rewording of a
statement, given in simple language for clarity. As a verb, *paraphrase*
means to render a paraphrase.

Example: The speaker talks about being worried that she has not
found an occupation that seems interesting. The listener responds:

"You seem nervous because you haven't found a job you want to do in the
future."

nervous = emotion word that describes the speaker's feelings
because you haven't found a job you want to do in the future = reason
for the feelings

Do not offer the speaker

- your advice ("You should . . . ")
- your opinion ("I think . . . ")
- your judgments ("That's crazy/stupid/weird")
- your life history ("Here's what happened to me . . . ")
- your predictions ("It/he/she will . . . ")

At first, listening and paraphrasing may feel uncomfortable because it is not
how we usually converse. But with a little practice you'll get good at it, and
those with whom you communicate—family, friends, lovers, and coworkers—will appreciate you greatly for it.

Reaction Essay

Respond in writing to the following questions.

1. With whom did you carry out the Listening Exercise?

2. In step 1, what topic did the speaker address?

3. In step 1, what did you notice your mind doing while the speaker was
   talking?

4. In step 4, what was the topic of the speaker's remarks?

5. In step 4, write the paraphrase you offered the speaker, using the
   speaker's emotion word (not yours!) and the speaker's because
   statement (not yours!).

   Correct: "You're nervous because you cannot find a job you want to do."
   Incorrect: "The speaker was nervous about not finding a job."
   Incorrect: "I was bored because I've heard this complaint a million
   times."

6. What effect did this exercise have on your usual listening style?

As a noun, the word *paraphrase* means a condensed rewording of a statement, given in simple language for clarity. As a verb, *paraphrase* means to
render a paraphrase.

9.1 Parenthood and Me

··

It's better to know some of the questions than all of the answers.
—James Thurber

Directions
In the list below, indicate how strongly you agree with each motivation for becoming a parent. Can you add any motivations to the list?

Motivation	Strongly agree	Agree	Disagree
To have a child who looks like me			
To have child who will carry on the family name			
To have a child who will be successful			
To have someone to inherit my money or property			
To have someone who will regard me highly			
To have someone who will return my love			
To do something I know I can do well			
To feel pride in creating another human being			
To keep me young at heart			
To help me feel fulfilled			
To make my marriage happier			
To make me feel masculine/feminine			
To please my family and society			
To teach someone about the beauty of life			
To help someone grow and develop			
Other			
Other			

10.1 Contraception

I believe in looking reality straight in the eye and denying it.
—Garrison Keillor

Directions

Respond to the questions below for any contraceptive method you are considering using.

Check **Yes** or **No** for each of the following questions:	Yes	No
1. Have I had problems using this method before?	_____	_____
2. Have 1 or my partner ever become pregnant while using this method?	_____	_____
3. Am I afraid of using this method?	_____	_____
4. Would I really rather not use this method?	_____	_____
5. Will I or my partner have trouble remembering to use this method?	_____	_____
6. Will I or my partner have trouble using this method correctly?	_____	_____
7. Do I still have unanswered questions about this method?	_____	_____
8. Does this method make menstrual periods longer or more painful?	_____	_____
9. Does this method cost more than I can afford?	_____	_____
10. Could this method cause me or my partner to have serious complications?	_____	_____
11. Am I opposed to this method because of my religious or moral beliefs?	_____	_____
12. Is my partner opposed to this method?	_____	_____
13. Am I using this method without my partner's knowledge?	_____	_____
14. Will using this method embarrass my partner?	_____	_____
15. Will using this method embarrass me?	_____	_____
16. Will I or my partner enjoy intercourse less because of this method?	_____	_____
17. If this method interrupts lovemaking, will I avoid it?	_____	_____
18. Has a nurse or physician ever told me or my partner *not* to use this method?	_____	_____
19. Is there anything about my or my partner's personality that could lead me or my partner to use this method incorrectly?	_____	_____
20. Am I or is my partner at risk of being exposed to HIV or another STD if I use or my partner uses this method?	_____	_____

Most persons will have a few "yes" answers. "Yes" answers mean that problems might arise. If you have more than a few "yes" responses, you may want to talk with a physician, counselor, partner, or friend to help you decide whether to use this method or how to use it so that it will really be effective for you. In general, the more "yes" answers you have, the less likely you are to use this method consistently and correctly at every act of intercourse.

Source: Byer, C. O., Shainberg, L. W., & Galliano, G. (1999). *Dimensions of human sexuality.* Boston, MA: McGraw-Hill College, p. 455.

10.2 Choosing a Contraceptive

Love is giving someone the space to be the way they are—and the way they are not.
—Edmund Burke

Directions

Rate the contraceptives in the list below and give reasons for your choices.

Method	Very suitable	Suitable	Not suitable	Reasons
Abstinence	_____	_____	_____	_____
Condom (female)	_____	_____	_____	_____
Condom (male)	_____	_____	_____	_____
Diaphragm	_____	_____	_____	_____
Fertility awareness	_____	_____	_____	_____
Hormonal pill	_____	_____	_____	_____
Hormonal patch	_____	_____	_____	_____
Hormonal ring	_____	_____	_____	_____
Intrauterine device (IUD)	_____	_____	_____	_____
Progestin-only method	_____	_____	_____	_____
Spermicidal foam/gel	_____	_____	_____	_____
Tubal ligation	_____	_____	_____	_____
Vasectomy	_____	_____	_____	_____

11.1 AIDS and Me

A loving heart is the beginning of all knowledge.
—Thomas Carlysle

How has HIV/AIDS touched your life? Write a response to this question considering the following aspects:

1. Personal experience with someone with HIV/AIDS

2. Whether HIV/AIDS has affected your personal behaviors

3. The ways HIV/AIDS has affected your community and society

4. The ways the worldwide HIV/AIDS epidemic affects your life

12

12.1 My Vaccination Record

There is an alchemy in sorrow. It can be transmuted into wisdom,
which, if it does not bring joy, can yet bring happiness.
—Pearl Buck

Directions

Make a record of your vaccinations using the chart below.

Vaccine	Year initial series completed	Years revaccinated					
Diphtheria							
Hepatitis A							
Hepatitis B							
Influenza							
Measles							
Mumps							
Pertussis (whooping cough)							
Polio							
German measles (rubella)							
Tetanus							
Tuberculosis							
Other							

13

13.1 My Cancer Risks

Judge thyself with the judgment of sincerity, and thou will judge others with the judgment of charity.
—John Mitchell Mason

Directions

1. Go to the online assessment tool Your Disease Risk at the Harvard Center for Cancer Prevention (http://www.yourdiseaserisk.harvard.edu/).

2. Click the What Is Your Risk of Cancer? link.

3. Assess your risks for any three of the cancers listed here:

   Bladder
   Breast
   Cervix
   Colon
   Kidney
   Lung
   Skin
   Ovary
   Pancreas
   Prostate
   Stomach
   Uterus

13.2 My Environmental Cancer Risks

Never confuse movement with action.
—Ernest Hemingway

Many environmental factors are linked to cancer, including those in the list below.

Directions

1. Estimate your exposure to each potential carcinogen listed in the chart below.

2. Write down some ideas about how you could reduce your exposure to some of them.

Potential Carcinogen	Exposure			
	High	Moderate	Low	None
Personal cigarette smoking	_____	_____	_____	_____
Secondhand smoke	_____	_____	_____	_____
Smokeless tobacco	_____	_____	_____	_____
Asbestos (in old buildings, including schools)	_____	_____	_____	_____
Radon (a radioactive gas in soil)	_____	_____	_____	_____
Indoor solid fuel (wood, coal) burning	_____	_____	_____	_____
Photochemical smog (from cars)	_____	_____	_____	_____
Humanpapilloma virus	_____	_____	_____	_____
Human immunodeficiency virus	_____	_____	_____	_____
Hepatitis B virus	_____	_____	_____	_____
Epstein-Barr virus	_____	_____	_____	_____
Helicobacter pylori infection	_____	_____	_____	_____
Sun exposure (or artificial tanning)	_____	_____	_____	_____
Well-done cooked meats	_____	_____	_____	_____
Postmenopausal estrogen therapy	_____	_____	_____	_____
Diethylstilbestrol (DES)	_____	_____	_____	_____
Benzene	_____	_____	_____	_____
Formaldehyde	_____	_____	_____	_____
Nickle-containing materials	_____	_____	_____	_____
Gamma irradiation	_____	_____	_____	_____
X-rays	_____	_____	_____	_____
Radioactive chemicals	_____	_____	_____	_____
Dioxin	_____	_____	_____	_____
Vinyl chloride	_____	_____	_____	_____
Coal tars	_____	_____	_____	_____
Soot	_____	_____	_____	_____
Wood dust	_____	_____	_____	_____

14

14.1 My Risk for Heart Disease

I don't know the key to success, but the key to failure is trying to please everybody.
—Bill Cosby

Directions

1. Go to the online assessment tool, Your Disease Risk, at the Harvard Center for Disease Prevention (http://www.yourdiseaserisk.harvard.edu/)

2. Click on "What Is Your Heart Disease Risk?"

3. Do the Questionnaire.

4. List any risk factors that you could/should lower, and for each, identify one health behavior you could change that would help reduce that risk.

15

15.1 My Family Medical History

Get your facts first, and then you can distort them as much as you please.
—Mark Twain

Directions

1. In the chart below, mark an "X" in a column to indicate the occurrence of a particular disease in a family member.

	Disease						If deceased, age at death	Cause of death
	Cancer	Diabetes	Heart disease	Hypertension	Stroke	Other		
Father								
Mother								
Brother								
Brother								
Sister								
Sister								
Father's father								
Father's mother								
Father's brother or sister								
Mother's father								
Mother's mother								
Mother's brother or sister								

2. For any "X" in your chart, research any possibility that the disease has some degree of heritability.

16

16.1 Being Knowledgeable About Drugs

When you win, say nothing. When you lose, say less.
—Paul Brown

What do you know about the drugs and medicines that you consume?

Directions

1. Go to one of the Web sites listed on this page (or an authoritative alternative) to learn about any medications or dietary supplements you are taking or have taken or a particular "recreational" or social drug you currently use or once used.

2. Describe something of interest that you learned.

_____

_____

_____

_____

Medicines

MedlinePlus Drug Information http://www.nlm.nih.gov/medlineplus/druginformation.html

Dietary Supplements

U.S. National Center for Complementary and Alternative Medicine http://nccam.nih.gov/health/supplements.htm

Nonmedical Drug Use

U.S. National Institute on Drug Abuse http://www.nida.nih.gov/

Alcohol Use and Abuse

U.S. National Institute on Alcohol Abuse and Alcoholism http://www.niaaa.nih.gov/

16.2 Medicines I Take

Do not throw the arrow which will return against you.
—Kurdish proverb

Directions

1. In the chart below, list any medicines you are taking. Consult the product packaging, your doctor, the pharmacist, authoritative books (e.g., *Physician's Desk Reference*), or the Internet for information about side effects and reasons not to take the medicine *(contraindications)*.

2. Assess the risks of taking a medicine in relation to its therapeutic benefits.

    _____

    _____

3. Search for nondrug alternatives to the drugs on your list.

    _____

    _____

Drug	Side effects	Contraindications

16.3 Nonessential Drugs I Consume

Of all forms of caution, caution in love is perhaps the most fatal to true happiness.
—Bertrand Russell

Americans consume too many drugs, in part because of the belief (promoted by drug manufacturers) that health and well-being are enhanced by chemicals. Whereas many drugs, when used appropriately, can promote wellness and relieve illness, too often people consume drugs unnecessarily.

Directions

1. For one week, make a list of the nonessential drugs you ingest. Be sure to include coffee, tea, and cola and "energy" drinks, all of which contain caffeine; alcohol, nicotine, and pain relievers.

2. After recording your nonessential drug consumption during Week 1, for another week try to eliminate one of the nonessential drugs you ingest and make notes about how you feel.

Week 1	Sun	Mon	Tues	Wed	Thurs	Fri	Sat
Caffeine (How many cups of coffee or 12-oz. servings of cola drinks per day?)							
Alcohol (How many 12-oz. beers, glasses of wine, or mixed drinks per day?)							
Nicotine (How many cigarettes, cigars, pipes, or dips of snuff or chewing tobacco per day?)							
Pain relievers (How many tablets per day?)							
Other:							
Other:							

Week 2	Sun	Mon	Tues	Wed	Thurs	Fri	Sat
Caffeine (How many cups of coffee or 12-oz. servings of cola drinks per day?)							
Alcohol (How many 12-oz. beers, glasses of wine, or mixed drinks per day?)							
Nicotine (How many cigarettes, cigars, pipes, or dips of snuff or chewing tobacco per day?)							
Pain relievers (How many tablets per day?)							
Other:							
Other:							

16.4 Drugs in Media and Advertising

Make the most of yourself, for that is all there is of you.
—Ralph Waldo Emerson

Directions

Find two examples of advertising in magazines, newspapers, radio, film, TV, or the Web that promote or facilitate the use of alcohol, tobacco, or prescription and nonprescription drugs. For each example, write an analysis in which you do the following:

1. Describe the images in the advertisement (e.g., the ages, appearance, and activities of the models; if a story is being depicted)

   _____

   _____

2. Identify the means by which the advertiser links the images in the ad to the product being sold

   _____

   _____

3. Identify the audience to which the ad is directed and how the imagery is used to "grab" that audience

   _____

   _____

4. Offer your opinion of the commercial effectiveness of the ad (i.e., does it sell?)

   _____

   _____

   _____

   _____

5. Offer your opinion of the effect of the ad on society

   _____

   _____

   _____

   _____

17

17.1 Why Do I Smoke?

To be conscious that you are ignorant is a great step to knowledge.
—Benjamin Disraeli

Smoking can provide a variety of rewards. Knowing the reasons you smoke can help you quit and stay smoke-free. Visit this page for more information on how to quit: http://health.jbpub.com/hwonline/9e/workbook/smoking.cfm

Directions

1. Answer the 18 questions below.

2. Use the scoring section to calculate your score for each of the smoking categories.

3. Consult the scoring interpretation page to find out what your scores mean.

	Always	Frequently	Occasionally	Seldom	Never
A. I smoke cigarettes to keep myself from slowing down.	5	4	3	2	1
B. Handling a cigarette is part of the enjoyment of smoking it.	5	4	3	2	1
C. Smoking cigarettes is pleasant and relaxing.	5	4	3	2	1
D. I light up a cigarette when I feel angry about something.	5	4	3	2	1
E. When I have run out of cigarettes I find it almost unbearable until I can get them.	5	4	3	2	1
F. I smoke cigarettes automatically without even being aware of it.	5	4	3	2	1
G. I smoke cigarettes to stimulate me, to perk myself up.	5	4	3	2	1
H. Part of the enjoyment of smoking a cigarette comes from the steps I take to light up.	5	4	3	2	1
I. I find cigarettes pleasurable.	5	4	3	2	1
J. When I feel uncomfortable or upset about something, I light up a cigarette.	5	4	3	2	1
K. I am very much aware of the fact when I am not smoking a cigarette.	5	4	3	2	1
L. I light up a cigarette without realizing I still have one burning in the ashtray.	5	4	3	2	1
M. I smoke cigarettes to give me a "lift."	5	4	3	2	1
N. When I smoke a cigarette, part of the enjoyment is watching the smoke as I exhale it.	5	4	3	2	1
O. I want a cigarette most when I am comfortable and relaxed.	5	4	3	2	1
P. When I feel "blue" or want to take my mind off cares and worries, I smoke cigarettes.	5	4	3	2	1
Q. I get a real gnawing hunger for a cigarette when I haven't smoked for a while.	5	4	3	2	1
R. I've found a cigarette in my mouth and didn't remember putting it there.	5	4	3	2	1

Source: Smoker's Self-Testing Kit developed by Daniel Horn, Ph.D. Originally published by National Clearinghouse for Smoking and Health. Department of Health, Education, and Welfare.

How to Score

1. Enter the numbers you have circled in the spaces below, putting the number you have circled to question A over line A, to question B over line B, etc.

2. Add the three scores on each line to get your totals. For example, the sum of your scores over lines A, G, and M gives you your score on *Stimulation,* lines B, H, and N give the score on *Handling,* and so on.

Totals

_____	+	_____	+	_____	=	_____
A		G		M		Stimulation
_____	+	_____	+	_____	=	_____
B		H		N		Handling
_____	+	_____	+	_____	=	_____
C		I		O		Pleasurable relaxation
_____	+	_____	+	_____	=	_____
D		J		P		Crutch: tension reduction
_____	+	_____	+	_____	=	_____
E		K		Q		Craving: psychological addiction
_____	+	_____	+	_____	=	_____
F		L		R		Habit

Scores of 11 or above indicate that this factor is an important source of satisfaction for the smoker. Scores of 7 or less are low and probably indicate that this factor does not apply to you. Scores in between are marginal. A description of what your scores mean can be found on the next page.

What My Scores Mean

Scores can vary from 3 to 15 in each category. A score of 11 or above is high; a score of 7 or less is low.

Stimulation

Smoking stimulates/energizes you. You believe smoking helps you wake up, concentrate, organize your energies, and keep going. If you scored more than 11 in this category, you need to find other ways to feel energized, such as the following:

- Avoid fatigue: get sufficient sleep so you won't feel tired.

- Take a walk (or do other exercise) to get yourself moving.

- Meditate to clear your mind and prepare yourself for a day's activities.

- Do some yoga or stretching exercises to balance your energy.

- Use a journal to plan your day's activities.

- Talk to someone or log on to a chat room.

- Chew cinnamon gum (or another strong flavor) to stimulate your sense of taste.

Handling

You like to handle cigarettes, a lighter, or matches. If you scored more than 11 in this category, you need to find other ways to satisfy your desire to handle things, such as the following:

- Hold a special object that has healing significance for you (a stone, beads, etc.).

- Hold a pen or pencil (or plastic cigarette).

- Doodle.

- Play with a coin, a piece of jewelry, or some other harmless object.

- Clean and polish your nails.

Pleasure

Smoking gives you pleasure (or reduces unpleasant feelings). If you scored more than 11 in this category, you need to find alternative ways to feel pleasure, such as the following:

- Meditate.

- Do a pleasurable activity.

- Remind yourself of the harmful effects of smoking.

- Chew a flavored gum that you like.

- Talk to someone or log on to a chat room.

Reduction of negative feelings or crutch

Smoking helps you cope with uncomfortable feelings and stress. If you scored more than 11 in this category, you need to find alternative ways to deal with unpleasant feelings, such as the following:

- Meditate.

- Write your thoughts and feelings in a journal.

- Talk to someone about your feelings.

- Take a walk or exercise.

- Listen to music.

- Identify common stressful situations in your life and experiment with nonsmoking coping methods to find ones that work best.

Craving

You experience cravings for cigarettes. If you scored more than 11 in this category, you need to find other ways to cope with cravings, such as the following:

- Become mindful of—and avoid—situations and circumstances that "trigger" smoking.

- Use deep breathing or meditation to help you let cravings pass.

- Use nicotine replacement products (patch or gum).

- Use craving-reducing medications (e.g., buproprion).

- Take soothing baths or showers.

Habit

For you, smoking is virtually automatic. You do it without thinking. If you scored more than 11 in this category, you need to replace smoking-related habits with nonsmoking ones, such as the following:

- Remove ash trays, cigarettes, and other smoking-related paraphernalia from your house, office, and car so they won't trigger automatic/mindless smoking.

- Designate smoke-free places in your home and office; make your car smoke-free.

- Sit in nonsmoking sections of restaurants.

- Don't go to bars and other locales that permit (and encourage) smoking.

- Make a pact with friends and coworkers who smoke not to smoke around you.

17.2 Am I Addicted to Nicotine?

I have come to believe that the whole world is an enigma, a harmless enigma that is made terrible by our own mad attempt to interpret it as though it had an underlying truth.

—Umberto Eco

Nicotine addiction (also called physical dependence) is a major reason for tobacco addiction. Without nicotine, a tobacco-addicted person experiences withdrawal syndrome consisting of being grouchy and irritable, having headaches, having trouble sleeping, having feeling depressed, and having intense cravings for cigarettes.

Directions

- For questions 1–6, circle the answer that best represents you.

- Add your points in column 3.

- Refer to the scoring section below to determine your level of nicotine addiction.

Questions	Answers	Points
1. How soon after you wake do you smoke your first cigarette?	Within 5 minutes	3
	6 to 30 minutes	2
2. Do you find it difficult to refrain from smoking in places where it is forbidden (e.g., in church, at the library, at the movies)?	Yes	1
	No	0
3. Which cigarette would you most hate to give up?	The first one in the morning	1
	All others	0
	10 or less	0
4. How many cigarettes per day do you smoke?	11 to 20	1
	21 to 30	2
	31 or more	3
5. Do you smoke more frequently during the first hours after waking than during the rest of the day?	Yes	1
	No	0
6. Do you smoke if you are so ill that you are in bed most of the day?	Yes	1
	No	0

Scoring

0 to 2—very low dependence

3 to 4—low dependence

5—medium dependence

6 to 7—high dependence

8 to 10—very high dependence

Source: Reprinted with permission from Fagerström, K. O., Heatherton, T. F., & Kozlowski, L. T. (1991). Nicotine addiction and its assessment. *Ear, Nose, and Throat Journal, 1990, 69,* 763–765.

CHAPTER

18

18.1 My Alcohol Use

Every man is guilty of all the good he didn't do.
—Voltaire

The CRAFFT and AUDIT (Alcohol Use Disorders Identification Test) questionnaires were developed to identify persons whose alcohol consumption may be hazardous to their health.

Directions:

- Visit the Web sites listed below and do the online questionnaires.

- If your scores indicate a drinking problem, talk with your doctor or a counselor.

CRAFFT:

http://www.drugfree.org/Intervention/Quiz/CRAFFT_Quiz

AUDIT:

http://www.counseling.caltech.edu/drug/selftest/test1.html

18.2 Cutting Down on Drinking

If you do not wish to be prone to anger, do not feed the habit; give it nothing which may tend to its increase.
—Epictetus (A.D. 55–135)

Directions

1. Respond to these questions:

- Do you drink alone when you feel angry or sad?

  _____

  _____

- Does your drinking ever make you late for work?

  _____

  _____

- Does your drinking worry your family?

  _____

  _____

- Do you ever drink after telling yourself you won't?

  _____

  _____

- Do you ever forget what you did while you were drinking?

  _____

  _____

- Do you get headaches or have a hangover after you have been drinking?

  _____

  _____

If you answered yes to any of the questions, you may have a drinking problem. If you want to cut down on your drinking, follow these steps:

1. Write your reasons for cutting down or stopping.

   _____

   _____

2. Set a drinking goal.

   Choose a limit for how much you will drink. You may choose to cut down or not to drink at all. If you are cutting down, keep below these limits:

   - Women: No more than one drink a day
   - Men: No more than two drinks a day

Now write your drinking goal on a piece of paper. Put it where you can see it, such as on your refrigerator or bathroom mirror. Your paper might look like this:

My drinking goal

> I will start on this day _____.
> I will not drink more than _____ drinks in 1 day.
> I will not drink more than _____ drinks in 1 week.
> or
> I will stop drinking alcohol.

3. Keep a diary of your drinking. Write down every time you have a drink for three to four weeks.

Week:			
	No. of Drinks	Type of Drinks	Place Consumed
Mon			
Tues			
Wed			
Thurs			
Fri			
Sat			
Sun			

Now you know why you want to drink less and you have a goal. There are many ways you can help yourself to cut down. Try the tips.

4. Watch it at home.

Keep a small amount or no alcohol at home. Don't keep temptations around.

5. Drink slowly.

When you drink, sip your drink slowly. Take a break of 1 hour between drinks. Drink soda, water, or juice after a drink with alcohol. Do not drink on an empty stomach! Eat food when you are drinking.

6. Take a break from alcohol.

Pick a day or two each week when you will not drink at all. Then, try to stop drinking for one week. Think about how you feel physically and emotionally on these days. When you succeed and feel better, you may find it easier to cut down for good.

7. Learn how to say *NO*.

You do not have to drink when other people drink. You do not have to take a drink that is given to you. Practice ways to say *no* politely. For example, you can tell people you feel better when you drink less. Stay away from people who give you a hard time about not drinking.

8. Stay active.

9. Get support.

Cutting down on your drinking may be difficult at times. Ask your family and friends for support to help you reach your goal. Talk to your doctor if you are having trouble cutting down. Get the help you need to reach your goal.

10. Watch out for temptations.

Watch out for people, places, or times that make you drink when you do not want to. Stay away from people who drink a lot or bars where you used to go. Plan ahead of time what you will do to avoid drinking when you are tempted.

Do not drink when you are angry or upset or have a bad day. These are habits you need to break if you want to drink less.

11. Do not give up!

Most people do not cut down or give up drinking all at once. Just like a diet, it is not easy to change. That is okay. If you do not reach your goal the first time, try again. Remember, get support from people who care about you and want to help.

Source: National Institute on Alcohol Abuse and Alcoholism, National Institutes of Health, March 1996, NIH Publication No. 96-3770.

19.1 My Medical History

If you can find a path with no obstacles, it probably doesn't lead anywhere.
—Frank A. Clark

As you are likely to have more than one health care provider in your life (thus increasing the risk of record-keeping errors), use the charts below to keep (and update regularly) your own medical records.

Illness History

Illness	No	Yes	When	Treatment	Special problems
German measles					
Mumps					
Chicken pox					
Scarlet fever					
Diphtheria					
Pneumonia, bronchitis, asthma					
Arthritis					
Rheumatic fever					
Heart disease or heart murmur					
Anemia					
Bleeding problem					
Ulcer, colitis					
Epilepsy					
Severe headaches					
Mononucleosis					
Jaundice or hepatitis					
Eye injury					
Ear disease or injury					
Skin disease					
Varicose veins					
Kidney or bladder problem					

Surgical History

What	When	Where	Physician

19.2 Am I an Intelligent Health Consumer?

Every increased possession loads us with new weariness.
—John Ruskin

This exercise can help you determine the extent to which you act intelligently when exposed to misleading and inaccurate health information, health fraud, and health quackery.

Directions
Place an *X* in the column that best represents your answer.

	VM	M	S	L	N
Are you sufficiently informed to be able to make sound decisions?					
Where do you go for information when needed?					
Professional health organizations or individuals					
Health books, magazines, newsletters					
Government health agencies					
Advertisements					
Newspapers or magazines					
Radio or television					
People you know					
To what extent do you accept statements appearing in news reports or advertisements at face value?					
To what extent can you identify quacks, quackery, fraudulent schemes, and hucksters?					
When selecting health practitioners to what extent do you:					
Talk with or visit before first appointment					
Check or inquire regarding qualifications or credentials					
Ask friend or neighbor about reputation					
Inquire about fees and payment procedures					
When you have been exposed to a fraudulent practice, quack, quackery, or a poor product or service, to what extent do you report your experience?					

Key: VM = very much; *M* = much; *S* = some; *L* = little; *N* = none.

Source: Comacchia, H. J., & Barrett, S. (1993). *Consumer health:* A guide in intelligent decisions (5th ed.). St. Louis, MO: Mosby, p. 11.

19.3 Using the Internet for Health Research

Words that come from the heart enter the heart.
—The Sages

Your tax dollars are definitely at work at the U.S. National Library of Medicine (part of the U.S. Department of Health and Human Services), the most comprehensive medical library in the world. One of the library's services is providing consumers with accurate, up-to-date, authoritative health and medical information through its MedlinePlus Web site: http://www.medlineplus.gov.

Directions

1. Visit the MedlinePlus Web site and click any links that interest you.

2. Describe your experience.

_____

_____

_____

_____

_____

_____

19.4 Web Field Trips

*You gain strength, courage, and confidence by every experience in which you
really stop to look fear in the face. You must do the thing which you think you
cannot do.*
—Eleanor Roosevelt

There are more than 10,000 health-related Web sites. The purpose of most of
them is to sell you something. A few health-related Web sites are not commercial; they are dedicated to providing authoritative health information to
help people. The purpose of the Web Field Trips exercise is to help you assess
health-related Web sites to determine those that are most authoritative, reliable, and helpful.

Directions

Visit, evaluate, and write a review of three health-related Web sites. The review should evaluate each Web site by addressing these questions:

1. What is the purpose of the Web site?

    _____

    _____

2. What does the site contain?

    _____

    _____

3. Who is responsible for the Web site's content?

    _____

    _____

4. How is the Web site funded and does the sponsorship influence the
    site's content?

    _____

    _____

5. How well is the Web site constructed?

    _____

    _____

6. How well does the Web site fulfill its purpose?

    _____

    _____

A list (with links) of authoritative health Web sites is on the *Health and
Wellness* Web site (http://health.jbpub.com/hwonline/9e/workbook/field-
trip.cfm). The list includes Web sites in the following categories:

Comprehensive Health Web sites	Nutrition
Mental Health	Alcohol and Drug Use and Abuse
Cancer	Human Genetics
Sexuality and Reproductive Health	Ear and Eye
Respiratory System and Allergy	Digestive System and Liver
Brain and Nervous System	Bones and Joints

20.1 Exploring Complementary and Alternative Medicine

I've missed more than 9,000 shots in my career. I've lost almost 300 games. Twenty-six times, I've been trusted to take the game winning shot and missed. I've failed over and over and over again in my life. And that is why I succeed.

—Michael Jordan

Directions

1. Visit the Web site of the National Center for Complementary and Alternative Medicine (http://nccam.nih.gov/), a division of the U.S. National Institutes of Health (NIH).

2. On the home page, click the link Making Decisions About Using CAM, and write a paragraph summary on what you find.

3. Browse the Web site and write a paragraph describing something of interest that you discover.

21.1 Preventing Intentional Injury

When I do good, I feel good; when I do bad, I feel bad, and that is my religion.
—Abraham Lincoln

Directions
Answer the questions in number 1 below and then respond to 2 and 3.

1. Answer *yes* or *no* to the following questions.

1. I have guns in my home.	Y	N
If yes, are they stored safely?	Y	N
When used, are they always used safely?	Y	N
2. I am involved in an abusive relationship.	Y	N
3. I five in a heavy-crime area.	Y	N
4. I abuse alcohol or other drugs.	Y	N
5. I work in a high-risk job.	Y	N
6. I clearly communicate my intentions and boundaries in a dating situation.	Y	N
7. I know, and have immediate access to, emergency phone numbers.	Y	N
8. I have sources of personal support.	Y	N
9. I know the warning signs of suicide.	Y	N
10. I know resources for mental health counseling in my community.	Y	N

2. Based on your responses to the questions in question 1, are there behaviors or situations in your life that need to be addressed? If so, what are they?

   _____

   _____

   _____

   _____

   _____

3. What concerns do you have, both as an individual and a member of your community, related to intentional injury and death?

   _____

   _____

   _____

   _____

   _____

Source: Birch and Creary. *Managing your health: Assessment and action.* © 1996 by Jones and Bartlett Publishers, Inc.

21.2 Preventing Unintentional Injury

Hate no one; hate their vices, not themselves.
—J. G. C. Brainard

Directions

Answer the questions in number 1 below and then respond to 2 and 3.

1. Answer *yes* or *no* to the following questions.

    1. I abuse alcohol or other drugs.   Y   N
    2. I wear seat belts when driving or riding in a car.   Y   N
    3. I have a car with front air bags.   Y   N
    4. I drive defensively rather than competitively.   Y   N
    5. I drive appropriately for weather conditions.   Y   N
    6. I maintain my car's tires, wipers, brakes, and lights.   Y   N
    7. I wear a helmet when riding on a bicycle, motorcycle, or roller blades.   Y   N
    8. I follow safety rules when riding a bicycle.   Y   N
    9. I keep gasoline, paint, oily rags, newspapers, plastics, and other flammable materials away from sources of heat.   Y   N
    10. I avoid overloading electrical circuits.   Y   N
    11. I use only safe sources of heat in my living quarters.   Y   N
    12. I avoid smoking in bed.   Y   N
    13. I have a smoke detector on each floor of my house.   Y   N
    14. I have a fire extinguisher in my house.   Y   N
    15. I keep a first-aid kit at home and in my car.   Y   N
    16. I post local emergency numbers and the poison control center number.   Y   N
    17. I follow safety procedures when involved in recreational activities.   Y   N

2. Based on your responses to the questions in question 1, are there behaviors or situations in your life that need to be addressed?

_____

_____

_____

3. What concerns do you have, both as an individual and a member of the community, related to unintentional injury and death?

_____

_____

_____

22.1 Healthy Aging

A great many people think they are thinking when they are really rearranging their prejudices.
—Edward R. Murrow

The health habits you observe as a young and middle-aged adult will greatly determine your health as an older person.

Directions

1. Indicate how frequently you practice each of the health behaviors listed below.

2. Among the health behaviors you do you not practice regularly, choose one that you could work on this year to make it a regular part of your life.

Frequency	Frequency		
	Regularly	Once in a while	Rarely
Do not smoke	_____	_____	_____
Consume recommended amount of fiber	_____	_____	_____
Consume recommended amount of calcium	_____	_____	_____
Consume five servings of fruits and vegetables per day	_____	_____	_____
Limit consumption of well-done meat	_____	_____	_____
Maintain normal body weight	_____	_____	_____
Practice physical activity 3–4 times a week	_____	_____	_____
Have social relationships and ties	_____	_____	_____
Have daily quiet time	_____	_____	_____
Consume minimal or no alcohol	_____	_____	_____
Consume minimal or no fast food	_____	_____	_____
Brush teeth twice a day	_____	_____	_____
Floss teeth once a day	_____	_____	_____
Obtain flu shots	_____	_____	_____
Obtain mammograms (if over age 40)	_____	_____	_____
Obtain Pap smear	_____	_____	_____
Practice humanpapilloma virus prevention	_____	_____	_____
Practice AIDS prevention	_____	_____	_____
Obtain colorectal screening (if over age 50)	_____	_____	_____
Obtain blood pressure screening	_____	_____	_____
Obtain cholesterol check screening	_____	_____	_____

23.1 Do I Protect Myself from Crime?

Whatever you do will be insignificant, but it is very important that you do it.
—Mahatma Gandhi

Crime Protection

Rate yourself on a scale of 1 to 5 to show how often you follow these crime prevention methods.

1 = always
2 = frequently
3 = sometimes
4 = rarely
5 = never

_____ 1. I walk in well-lit areas.
_____ 2. I watch where I am going and what is happening to me.
_____ 3. I try to avoid walking alone at night.
_____ 4. I carry a whistle in my hand when walking alone.
_____ 5. I lock my car doors and do not leave valuables in sight.
_____ 6. I get out my car keys before I reach my car.
_____ 7. I park in well-lit and well-traveled areas of the parking lot.
_____ 8. I know the location of campus pay phones and call boxes.
_____ 9. I always carry cash in case of an emergency.
_____ 10. I avoid working or studying in buildings alone.
_____ 11. I take the safest, not the fastest, route when walking on campus.
_____ 12. I use shuttle buses or a campus escort service after dark.
_____ 13. I have memorized the phone number of the campus police.
_____ 14. When jogging or biking, I go with a friend and exercise on well-traveled routes.
_____ 15. If strangers harassed me, I would leave the scene and go to an open store, gas station, or anywhere people are present.
_____ 16. If I were held up, I would give the perpetrator my possessions and not fight.
_____ 17. If I were assaulted, I would try not to panic and look at the attacker carefully in order to give a good description to police.

Adapted from Ball State University's Campus Safety Tips (www.bsu.edu), Las Positas College's Campus Crime Prevention Web site (www.laspositascollege.edu), and information from the Columbus, Ohio, Police Department (www.columbuspolice.org).

24

24.1 Environmental Awareness Questionnaire

Success usually comes to those who are too busy to be looking for it.
—Henry David Thoreau

Directions

Circle the number that is your most appropriate response to each question.
Do you use pesticides in the house to kill insects, such as ants, roaches, or flies?

1. Frequently

2. Occasionally

3. Almost never

Do you use pesticides or herbicides around the garden and yard to kill insects and weeds?

1. Frequently

2. Occasionally

3. Almost never

Do you recycle newspapers or other kinds of paper?

1. Almost never

2. Sometimes

3. Regularly

Do you recycle bottles, cans, or plastics?

1. Hardly ever recycle these items

2. Some of these items sometimes

3. Most of the items regularly

When you go on a picnic or hike do you pack up and dispose of all trash in proper trash receptacles?

1. Very infrequently

2. Sometimes

3. All the time

If you need to run an errand that is less than a half mile away, do you walk or bike instead of drive?

1. Almost never

2. Occasionally

3. Most of the time

Do you conserve electricity by turning off unneeded lights and by not running appliances when you don't really need to (like the air conditioner)?

1. Hardly ever

2. Some of the time

3. Almost always

Do you make an effort to conserve water when showering, flushing, washing the car, etc.?

1. Almost never

2. Sometimes

3. Almost always

Do you pour dangerous chemicals such as gasoline or paint solvents down the drain or into sewer systems instead of arranging for proper disposal?

1. Often

2. Sometimes

3. Almost never

Have you thrown an empty can or bottle into the environment?

1. Within the past week

2. Within the past month

3. Not within the past year that you can remember

If you smoke, do you throw your butts into the environment when smoking outside?

1. Usually

2. Occasionally

3. Never

What kind of mileage does your automobile average?

1. Less than 20 miles per gallon

2. 20 to 30 miles per gallon

3. More than 30 miles per gallon

If you play a radio outdoors, how loud do you play it?

1. About as loud as it will go

2. Just loud enough for me to hear

3. Never play a radio outdoors where it might disturb others

When shopping for needed products, do you look for environmentally safe ones?

1. Never, just look for the cheapest and best product

2. Sometimes, depends on what is needed

3. Almost always, if I can find one

How many motor vehicles do you own, including cars, motorcycles, motorboats, jet skis, and others?

1. More than four

2. Two to four

3. Only one

A perfect score on these specific environmental questions is 45, but remember that no one is perfect. Perhaps by reviewing your answers you can find ways to improve your environmental awareness—and also contribute to your own health.

24.2 How Environmentally Friendly Is My Car?

Do not condemn the judgment of another because it differs from your own. You may both be wrong.
—Dandemis

Directions

1. Go to the U.S. Department of Energy's air pollution Web site (http://www.fueleconomy.gov).

2. Click the link at the upper left called Find and Compare Cars and report the annual greenhouse gas emissions in tons per year and the air pollution score (if given) of your current car. (If you don't drive a car, acquire the data for the car of someone you know.)

3. Compare the greenhouse gas emissions and air pollution scores of your present car with your prior car. Any improvements?

24.3 How Healthy Is My Drinking Water?

Arithmetic is being able to count up to twenty without taking off your shoes.
—Mickey Mouse

The Environmental Protection Agency sets health standards for drinking water. Obtain a report from your local water supplier's most recent report on the quality of the water distributed to you. The easiest way to do this is to contact your local water system (phone or e-mail) and ask. An alternative is to use the EPA Web site: http://www.epa.gov/safewater/dwinfo/index.html.